If you wish, initial in a space to
indicate you've read this book

René Lévesque

ALSO IN THE
EXTRAORDINARY CANADIANS
SERIES:

Big Bear by Rudy Wiebe
Lord Beaverbrook by David Adams Richards
Norman Bethune by Adrienne Clarkson
Emily Carr by Lewis DeSoto
Tommy Douglas by Vincent Lam
Glenn Gould by Mark Kingwell
Louis-Hippolyte LaFontaine and Robert Baldwin
by John Ralston Saul
Wilfrid Laurier by André Pratte
Stephen Leacock by Margaret MacMillan
Nellie McClung by Charlotte Gray
Marshall McLuhan by Douglas Coupland
L.M. Montgomery by Jane Urquhart
Lester B. Pearson by Andrew Cohen
Maurice Richard by Charles Foran
Mordecai Richler by M.G. Vassanji
Louis Riel and Gabriel Dumont by Joseph Boyden
Pierre Elliott Trudeau by Nino Ricci

SERIES EDITOR:
John Ralston Saul

René Lévesque

by Daniel Poliquin

With an Introduction by
John Ralston Saul
SERIES EDITOR

EXTRAORDINARY
CANADIANS

PENGUIN CANADA

Published by the Penguin Group

Penguin Group (Canada), 90 Eglinton Avenue East, Suite 700, Toronto, Ontario, Canada M4P 2Y3
(a division of Pearson Canada Inc.)

Penguin Group (USA) Inc., 375 Hudson Street, New York, New York 10014, U.S.A.
Penguin Books Ltd, 80 Strand, London WC2R 0RL, England
Penguin Ireland, 25 St Stephen's Green, Dublin 2, Ireland (a division of Penguin Books Ltd)
Penguin Group (Australia), 250 Camberwell Road, Camberwell, Victoria 3124, Australia
(a division of Pearson Australia Group Pty Ltd)
Penguin Books India Pvt Ltd, 11 Community Centre, Panchsheel Park, New Delhi – 110 017, India
Penguin Group (NZ), 67 Apollo Drive, Rosedale, North Shore 0745, Auckland, New Zealand
(a division of Pearson New Zealand Ltd)
Penguin Books (South Africa) (Pty) Ltd, 24 Sturdee Avenue, Rosebank,
Johannesburg 2196, South Africa

Penguin Books Ltd, Registered Offices: 80 Strand, London WC2R 0RL, England

First published 2009

1 2 3 4 5 6 7 8 9 10 (RRD)

Copyright © Daniel Poliquin, 2009
Introduction copyright © John Ralston Saul, 2009

Manufactured in the U.S.A.

LIBRARY AND ARCHIVES CANADA CATALOGUING IN PUBLICATION

Poliquin, Daniel
René Lévesque / Daniel Poliquin.

(Extraordinary Canadians)
Includes bibliographical references.
ISBN 978-0-670-06919-4

1. Lévesque, René, 1922-1987. 2. Québec (Province)—History—Autonomy
and independence movements. 3. Québec (Province)—Politics and government—
1976-1985. 4. Québec (Province)—Politics and government—1960-1976.
5. Parti québecois—Biography. 6. Prime ministers—Québec (Province)—Biography.
I. Title. II. Series: Extraordinary Canadians

FC2925.1.L5P64 2009   971.4'04'092   C2009-902417-9

Visit the Penguin Group (Canada) website at **www.penguin.ca**

Special and corporate bulk purchase rates available; please see
www.penguin.ca/corporatesales or call 1-800-810-3104, ext. 477 or 474

This book was printed on 30% PCW recycled paper

CONTENTS

CONTENTS

John Ralston Saul

How do civilizations imagine themselves? One way is for each of us to look at ourselves through our society's most remarkable figures. I'm not talking about hero worship or political iconography. That is a danger to be avoided at all costs. And yet people in every country do keep on going back to the most important people in their past.

This series of Extraordinary Canadians brings together rebels, reformers, martyrs, writers, painters, thinkers, political leaders. Why? What is it that makes them relevant to us so long after their deaths?

For one thing, their contributions are there before us, like the building blocks of our society. More important than that are their convictions and drive, their sense of what is right and wrong, their willingness to risk all, whether it be their lives, their reputations, or simply being wrong in public. Their ideas, their triumphs and failures, all of these somehow constitute a mirror of our society. We look at these people, all dead, and discover what we have been, but also what we can be. A mirror is an instrument for measuring ourselves. What we see can be both a warning and an encouragement.

These eighteen biographies of twenty key Canadians are centred on the meaning of each of their lives. Each of them is very different, but these are not randomly chosen great figures. Together they produce a grand sweep of the creation of modern Canada, from our first steps as a democracy in 1848 to our questioning of modernity late in the twentieth century.

All of them except one were highly visible on the cutting edge of their day while still in their twenties, thirties, and forties. They were young, driven, curious. An astonishing level of fresh energy surrounded them and still does. We in the twenty-first century talk endlessly of youth, but power today is often controlled by people who fear the sort of risks and innovations embraced by everyone in this series. A number of them were dead—hanged, infected on a battle-field, broken by their exertions—well before middle age. Others hung on into old age, often profoundly dissatisfied with themselves.

Each one of these people has changed you. In some cases you know this already. In others you will discover how through these portraits. They changed the way the world hears music, thinks of war, communicates. They changed how each of us sees what surrounds us, how minorities are treated, how we think of immigrants, how we look after each other, how we imagine ourselves through what are now our stories.

You will notice that many of them were people of the word. Not just the writers. Why? Because civilizations are built around many themes, but they require a shared public language. So Laurier, Bethune, Douglas, Riel, LaFontaine, McClung, Trudeau, Lévesque, Big Bear, even Carr and Gould, were masters of the power of language. Beaverbrook was one of the most powerful newspaper publishers of his day. Countries need action and laws and courage. But civilization is not a collection of prime ministers. Words, words, words—it is around these that civilizations create and imagine themselves.

The authors I have chosen for each subject are not the obvious experts. They are imaginative, questioning minds from among our leading writers and activists. They have, each one of them, a powerful connection to their subject. And in their own lives, each is engaged in building what Canada is now becoming.

That is why a documentary is being filmed around each subject. Images are yet another way to get at each subject and to understand their effect on us.

The one continuous, essential voice of biography since 1961 has been the *Dictionary of Canadian Biography*. But there has not been a project of book-length biographies such as Extraordinary Canadians in a hundred years, not since the Makers of Canada series. And yet every generation understands the past differently, and so sees in the mirror of these remarkable figures somewhat different lessons. As history rolls on, some truths remain the same while others are revealed in a new and unexpected way.

What strikes me again and again is just how dramatically ethical decisions figured in these people's lives. They form the backbone of history and memory. Some of them, Big Bear, for example, or Dumont, or even Lucy Maud Montgomery, thought of themselves as failures by the end of their lives. But the ethical cord that was strung taut through their work has now carried them on to a new meaning and even greater strength, long after their deaths.

Each of these stories is a revelation of the tough choices unusual people must make to find their way. And each of us as readers will find in the desperation of the Chinese revolution, the search for truth in fiction, the political and military dramas, different meanings that strike a personal chord. At first it is that personal emotive link to such figures which draws us in. Then we find they are a key that opens the whole society of their time to us. Then we realize that in that 150-year period many of them knew each other, were friends, opposed each other. Finally, when all these stories are put together, you will see that a whole new debate has been created around Canadian civilization and the shape of our continuous experiment.

Some of those who supported René Lévesque or opposed him in his mission to change Quebec, and therefore Canada, will ask what he is doing in a series devoted to Extraordinary Canadians. But that is precisely what he was—an egalitarian, deeply ethical man, a man who pointed his finger at whatever wasn't fair or inclusive in our society, a man who questioned Canadians in their assumptions about themselves.

He made Canada a more interesting place, arguably a better place. Across the country people identified with him and, quite simply, liked him, even when they completely disagreed with him. Daniel Poliquin, with his sharp skills as a novelist and essayist and political thinker, uncovers all of this. What Lévesque wanted as a social leader becomes perfectly clear. What he wanted as a political leader remains perfectly uncertain. In both cases, he added a great deal to our lives and to our country.

René Lévesque

CHAPTER ONE

Money Matters

When René Lévesque left politics in the fall of 1985, he handed his landlady the keys to the Quebec City flat he had rented during his nine years as premier. She asked him whether he had left anything behind. "No, no," he said, "I've got everything right in here." And he showed her the Provigo grocery bag he was holding on to.

Now, here was a man who had been in politics for twenty-five years; had founded a successful political party, the Parti Québécois (PQ); had been elected and re-elected premier of his province against formidable odds; had been instrumental in shaping his people's destiny as well as Canada's; and all he took back home could fit into a shopping bag.

René Lévesque's proverbial disregard for money was one of the many reasons people liked him so much. As a politician, he managed the public purse as well as he could, even originating some astounding successes—Hydro-Québec, for instance. But his PQ government was also blamed for some equally spectacular failures: the provincial takeover of

Quebec's asbestos mines, to name but one. Still, people believed in their heart of hearts that he was a man of impeccable integrity.

True, his rapport with money may have been conditioned by his socio-cultural makeup. Jesuit-schooled as he was, he had surely been taught to be wary of soul-corrupting wealth. As well, he grew up speaking French, a language amazingly resourceful at camouflaging the vileness of money, especially if you have some.

However, Lévesque was too much of a rebel to let social determinants such as these instill in him indifference to money. His prodigal son behaviour actually stemmed more from a deeply entrenched adolescent psyche. He was forever the teenager who did not have two red cents to rub together, oblivious to what tomorrow would bring. Hence, his incorrigible chain-smoking, all-night poker-playing, hard-drinking, and skirt-chasing habits. And, like any life-loving teen, he did not mind hard work as long as it was rewarded with heavy partying and late-morning sleep.

He took the same devil-may-care attitude to his sovereignty-association project, whereby Quebec would become a separate state while maintaining economic ties with Canada and, notably, keeping our very reassuring Canadian dollar. When told by economists that he could not have political independence without monetary self-sufficiency, he dismissed their objections as a mere matter of "plumbing." "We'll iron out the details later, things will take care of themselves …" The adolescent in him would never let what many thought were incontestable facts interfere with his political and economic reverie.

His distrust of coin and paper had developed early in his life. Growing up in the Gaspé Peninsula in the dirt-poor 1920s and 1930s, he saw first-hand how cash-strapped fishermen became ensnared in a system of neo-feudal exploitation. Rich local merchants would pay for the fish half in cash and half in goods sold at the company stores, which held a monopoly on fishing gear and staples like flour and molasses, all sold of course to captive customers at outrageous prices. As a result, most fishermen ended up indebted to the company for life. Memories of men selling their lobster catches for pennies at the local wharf remained etched in young René's mind. If money leads to economic serfdom, then money cannot be good, he reasoned. No wonder he found a feeling of emancipation in his disdain for wealth.

Sheer political will also contributed to shaping his outlook on money. Like all his contemporaries, Lévesque could see throughout his adulthood how slush funds greased political wheels in Quebec and elsewhere in Canada, with anonymous bagmen bullying elected officials in cigar-smoke-filled rooms, immune to any sort of political accountability. He could see it in the Union Nationale (UN) of Premier Maurice Duplessis, the elected strongman who governed his native province without paying much heed to the social injustices of the times. He could also witness it in his first political family, the Quebec Liberal Party (QLP), always careful not to step on the delicate toes of moneymen. So something had to be done to free politics from dirty money—and that he managed to do just that is surely his greatest feat as a politician and his most enduring legacy.

Thus, when Lévesque founded the Parti Québécois after bolting from the QLP in 1967, he made sure that no donor, corporate or individual, would ever hamper political freedom again. His party would belong to its members only. And when he finally reached power in 1976, the first legislation he passed outlawed the pollution of politics by unaccounted-for money.

But he was no ascetic figure, far from it: he enjoyed his two packs of Belvederes a day, his marathon card games, and his extra-arid martinis too much for that. He was in fact very comfortable with the lifestyle of the ageless bohemian. That was who he was. In the 1970s, visitors to his apartment on

Pine Avenue in Montreal would notice the shabby, butt-stained furniture and the milk crate dressed up as a coffee table. According to biographer Pierre Godin, the author of four well-researched tomes on Lévesque, the PQ leader's passbook at the caisse populaire showed a balance of $290.47 in December 1973, and the nest egg had melted to $76.54 in February 1974, just enough to buy a couple cartons of cigarettes and a bottle or two of château-dépanneur, the kind of plonk available at the nearby corner store.

His sartorial tastes confirmed his vow of indifference to all things material. He was probably the first and only premier-elect in Canada to show up at his swearing-in ceremony dressed like a man who lives from one paycheque to the next: a brown leather coat whose better days were long forgotten, an off-the-rack rumpled suit with a crooked tie, Wallabees, whatever little hair left dishevelled, a face like an unmade bed, a lit cigarette hanging from his lips. He did not look the part of the powerful premier he had just become; he simply looked like who he was: the René Lévesque everybody knew, who was the same in real life as he was in the media.

He looked real, and Canadians seemed to enjoy authenticity. We still do.

CHAPTER TWO

Heart Matters

We often overlook the role that feelings play in the everyday choices we make, politics included. Whether we call it the heart or the soul or just emotions, when it comes to voting for a candidate, a party, or a leader, we often willingly let what I call the "tolerated irrational within us" partly dictate our behaviour. Our feelings intervene because we are human beings, imperfect by nature—and we should be thankful that it is so. We are not guided solely by our intellect; we are not all dollars and cents, and we never fully understand how that mixture of aspirations and impulses will lead some of us to fall in love with strange-looking dogs or oddly shaped cars that result in gaping holes in our finances. The tolerated irrational within us may also account for the unrewarded fidelity of long-suffering Maple Leafs fans or the nostalgia inspired by eccentric public figures: a John Diefenbaker in politics or a Tiger Williams in hockey.

In the realm of politics, whether we like a candidate is as important as that candidate's platform. And when we make our final choice in the voting booth, intellect and information often take a back seat to instinct and immediate impressions. Likeability elicits trust, which perhaps explains why harmless but endearing nobodies often fare better in electoral matches than world-savvy academics.

People liked René Lévesque as a man and as a politician. And he liked people. They knew it in their bones and reciprocated. Blessed with an emotional quotient that must have been off the charts, he was the walking definition of political empathy. When embracing a cause, he was always visceral, and it showed in his body language and choice of vocabulary.

Before he entered politics, in his career as a broadcaster, he did not take long to secure the affection of listeners and viewers—probably because his speaking style was all instinct, no method. He could explain an issue with words that came straight from his heart, allowing his audience to understand it as well as he did. He always used words that everybody could understand without ever dumbing-down his treatment of the issues of the day. Many noted that he made people feel intelligent when he talked to them. Moreover, he never abused his powers as a wordsmith. After he entered politics, although he brought the same passion to his endeavours, he managed to maintain a rational composure that only reinforced the spontaneous trust he generated.

I once asked my aunt Marcelle, from Longueuil, Quebec, who would never vote PQ to save her life, why she liked Lévesque in spite of his sovereignty ideal. "Because he looked honest," she said. I put the same question to Martin, a colleague of mine. He said, "I liked him because he looked unsure of himself." "I beg your pardon?" "Yes," he explained, "it made him look human, and I never felt pressured to believe him. With him, I could remain free to think what I wanted." That may be the ultimate compliment you can pay a politician. Indeed, excessive self-confidence is never too good a thing in the political arena.

René Lévesque had seen too much of the world before entering politics, namely conflict-ravaged Europe in the final days of the Second World War and later the Korean War, not to be wary of absolute truths. Similarly, as a young man, Oliver Wendell Holmes of U.S. Supreme Court fame had witnessed the horrors of the Civil War at Antietam. And even though he had fought the good fight on the Union's side, he had come away with the feeling that certainty always leads to violence. Lévesque's own doubts were instrumental in quelling the violent episodes of his times.

Even his enemies enjoyed him, and his supporters in the PQ, whom he often disappointed with his changes of heart, were always forgiving, like the spouse willing to tolerate any infidelity. The English-speaking press fondly called him "René," seldom forgetting the acute accent (whereas they never used "Joe" for Prime Minister Clark, except to deride him), and the French-speaking media treated him as the former colleague he was: with respect and affection, sometimes at the expense of objectivity, until the twilight years of his career when things started to unravel for him.

Although he did not have matinee idol looks, women fawned over him, and he returned the attention with zeal. Endowed with an overpowering charisma and a winning way with words, he looked upon women as voters he had to charm into electing him.

And he was a talented vote-getter.

He was at his best handling a crowd, working magic with his words, and throngs were perhaps the only true love of his life.

But he was not a man you could get close to. Although he was very emotional at times, he did not wear his heart on his sleeve and had only contempt for his separatist rival, Pierre Bourgault, the leader of the Rassemblement pour l'indépendance nationale (RIN), who was all heart and no sleeve. He also distrusted Bourgault's oratorical skills, for he feared they might whip a crowd into a frenzy and unleash violent emotions. Lévesque's passion was visible, but he refrained from courting the bad angels of our nature.

He was also loved like a father figure by many supporters, and herein lies what is perhaps Lévesque's greatest paradox: he was much more a son-like figure, as evidenced by his life-wrecking habits and his political outlook. He was all right as a father to his three legitimate children but as cold as ice to the daughter he had outside marriage. And he hated being an ersatz father to anyone. To this day, however, he is regarded as the founding father of the modern nationalist movement, a sentiment that would have made him wince.

René Lévesque had only one serious rival in the affection of Quebecers: Pierre Elliott Trudeau, who was all empathy too, although he pretended it did not exist for him. The voters of Quebec loved both native sons so much that they chained them to the same ball throughout their respective careers. Much to their benefit, as it turned out.

ALTHOUGH RENÉ LÉVESQUE never appeared to exact love from anyone, he could not get enough of it. Human love just could not heal the wound he alone knew about.

This unquenchable thirst may have its origins on the date of his birth, August 24, 1922. In his memoirs, Lévesque states that in the eyes of the world around him, he was a fine-looking baby but reportedly not as cute as the first-born son of the family, whose neck had been broken by the drunk doctor assisting his mother at the home birth, nor as handsome as the brother who followed him. Not many sixty-three-year-old memoirists would admit to the existence of such an early longing for preference.

Diehard fans of René Lévesque hate hearing this, but their hero was not born in the province that he wanted to sever from Canada. His birthplace was actually the Hôtel-Dieu Hospital of Campbellton, New Brunswick, across Chaleur Bay from Quebec. The Lévesque family had settled in New Carlisle, in the Gaspé Peninsula, but they wanted to avoid another disastrous home birth. It was also to that sad episode that he owed his Christian name: René, the born again.

If your rank in the family has any bearing on your future, of René it can be safely said that he never acted like the classic first-born who sets high standards for the siblings and emulates the father in all his good deeds. Quite the opposite, René always acted like the son deprived of his birthright, bent on proving to the rest of the world that he was somebody, too. As if his phantom brother had never ceased to haunt him.

It was a good family. Both parents hailed from eminently respectable clans of the Lower St. Lawrence region. His mother, Diane Dionne, was the daughter of a doctor; her grandfather had been a doctor too. René's father, Dominique Lévesque, was a lawyer who had articled with Ernest Lapointe, MP and Attorney General of Canada, who was Mackenzie King's alter ego and Quebec lieutenant. Dominique was an enlightened gentleman who surrounded himself with books; to keep abreast of world events, he had two trees chopped down to have a makeshift radio antenna installed in his backyard. Young René was thus one of the few fortunate children in New Carlisle able to listen to the words and music of faraway worlds and to read whatever he pleased, which he did voraciously.

The family lived well. Dominique had come to New Carlisle at the invitation of the law firm headed by local magnate John Hall Kelly, owner of the Bonaventure and Gaspé Telephone Company and the *Gaspé Gazette,* who had an eminently successful but forgettable career in politics, ending up as Canada's High Commissioner in Dublin. The Lévesques were one of the few families in town to own a car and their own home, with a housekeeper to help with the chores and the raising of René and his three younger siblings. They subscribed to a number of periodicals, and mother and father were even able to afford a holiday in the south of France, quite the luxury in those days.

New Carlisle was then a mostly English-speaking town populated by descendants of Loyalists, which meant that René had to become bilingual at a very young age. He began his education in a one-room schoolhouse ruled by a Miss Gorman, who had the unenviable task of teaching a rowdy horde of children from grades one to six. The language of instruction was English, *naturellement.*

By all accounts, the boy was very intelligent and vivacious; a little pest too, who sometimes got the strap from his father. Not a cruel and unusual punishment in those days, and it certainly did not dim the fierce love he felt for his father and the fond memories he had of a Tom Sawyer–like childhood by the sea, with fishing, swimming, and occasional but inconsequential fisticuffs between *les Anglais* and *les Français,* who afterwards would resume their children's games together.

René Lévesque's bilingual upbringing, a very rare occurrence then in Quebec, was one of the traits he shared with his two most bitter enemies: the RIN's Pierre Bourgault, who grew up in East Angus in the Eastern Townships and also spoke English with near-native fluency, and, of course, the other Pierre: Trudeau, middle name Elliott.

CHAPTER THREE

Gaspé

René was eleven when he entered the Jesuit-run Séminaire de Gaspé in the fall of 1933. For higher schooling, his family did not have much choice. Any well-to-do French-Canadian family in those days would send the boys to the seminary, the girls to the convent. Education had been the Catholic Church's purview ever since the Quebec government, under pressure from conservative nationalists, had abolished its education ministry in 1875.

The curriculum was the same just about everywhere: eight years of Scripture, French grammar and literature, Latin, Greek, a tiny bit of English, some mathematics, some sciences, French-Canadian history to make a proud patriot out of you, a little geography and botany, sometimes astronomy, depending on the teaching resources available, and in later years a heavy load of theology and philosophy, often taught in Latin. There was virtually no physical education, but you could play hockey in the winter on the seminary's rink, with priests and brothers tying their cassocks around their waists in order to skate at ease. The library was usually of good standing—for those who enjoyed morally irreproachable authors. Of course, no Voltaire, no Victor Hugo, such writers being on the Index (that is, forbidden by Rome). No subscriptions to magazines or newspapers, either—except perhaps *Le Devoir,* if you were lucky—and the only newspaper clippings available were safe, dated accounts of sports news usually found in the lavatory.

The whole program was crowned by a Bachelor of Arts degree. The young men who survived it all could then study another four years for the priesthood or go to university where doctors and lawyers were trained. For young women, there was nursing school, teachers' college, becoming a nun, or marriage. Quebec's school system was woefully inadequate if you were drawn to economics, accounting, sciences, or technical trades. The priests and the nuns could, however, teach you how to write and speak. Not a bad thing if you were inclined to make a living in journalism and politics, for instance.

Life at the seminary was intense, especially for boarders like René. Prayer exercises were numerous and attendance at the daily morning mass was compulsory, as were regular trips to the confessional. Between classes, there was little time left for idle hands tempted by evil deeds. The food was bad, but you would not go hungry if you were not too choosy. Hygiene was kept to the basics, with the proverbial Saturday bath, just like at home. In the first two months kids would cry themselves to sleep because they missed their families so much. But if they could overcome the first pangs of loneliness and withstand the tedium of life as a budding cleric, many would do all right and form new, lasting ties. For years afterwards, the alumni would talk about those years with either fondness or revulsion, depending on their experience.

René did well at Gaspé. He got along with everybody, and his marks usually put him near the top of the class. He was also receptive to the ideological teachings of some Jesuit fathers, that is, nationalism. Very receptive, indeed. For instance, in May 1936 he wrote in the seminary's student paper, *L'envol:* "Let us reclaim from the Jews and the Americans the elevated positions that should be ours, instead of being content with the contemptible occupations we are left."

The boy was thirteen. He had never met a Jew or an American in his life. Isolated as he was from the real world, where could he have got such ideas? From the Black Robes, of course. The writings of Charles Maurras, France's nationalist firebrand, and of Quebec's own Canon Lionel Groulx, the self-appointed apostle of French Canada's grandeur, permeated virtually all the seminaries of Quebec in the 1930s, and the Gaspé seminary was no exception. Young René may have been a little zealous in wanting to please his masters, but he was only parroting what he was taught. He did not leave Gaspé a confirmed anti-Semite, however. For that matter, nor did his fellow students. Children who are force-fed thought often repudiate it later if they are of a generous nature, or they just plain forget it as useless "school stuff," or they do not take it in in the first place. (We must be thankful for all those students who do not always listen in class, who do not do their homework, or who are blessed with a weak memory: a lot of brainwashing gets tossed out that way.) Or life teaches you otherwise, and you remain suspicious of institutionalized learning for the rest of your life.

That is probably what happened to young René. It's certainly what happened to his confrere, three years older and also a bright pupil of the Jesuits in Montreal: Pierre Trudeau, who, for a while, spared no effort in pleasing his nationalist teachers. He wrote short plays in which stereotypical Jews were derided; he even wrote in his diary that he dreamed of liberating Quebec at the head of an army one day, in faraway 1976. Trudeau was thus a model student, surpassing his masters in fostering prejudices and in political fantasy. Then he went to Harvard, travelled, saw the world, tramped at the Sorbonne and at Oxford, met women, had fun, and threw all these teachings overboard for good. It was the same for Lévesque. Almost.

In Trudeau's case, the break with nationalism was more decisive after the Second World War and Harvard. He became nationalism's most ardent foe, whereas Lévesque remained a nationalist all his life. He would even write in Radio-Canada's *Journal interne* in 1948: "I am for all practical purposes a Quebec nationalist, a dyed-in-the-wool Laurentian [that is, a French-speaking inhabitant of the St. Lawrence Valley]." Fortunately, for him and for us, life experience had already diluted the potentially toxic convictions he acquired at the knees of the Good Fathers.

CHAPTER FOUR

Quebec City

Think of the majestic Chateau Frontenac, of the ramparts oozing history, of the tourist traps, the restaurants, and the hospitable inhabitants, of the much-vaunted European flavour of the ancient town, the province's very seat of power. Lévesque hated it.

Understandably so: Quebec City was the place where his family moved after his father died. His beloved father, his "hero" as he called him, had passed away in the aftermath of a botched operation, on June 18, 1937. René was fourteen, and his father had just found him his first summer job as a translator of news releases and replacement announcer with CHNC New Carlisle. Four months later, his mother had remarried: Albert Pelletier, a friend of the family and a lawyer with strong connections to the nationalist milieu. Lévesque instantly took a strong dislike to him and felt no gratitude for the new home in Quebec City, so far from the Gaspesian children's paradise.

As the French philosopher Jean-Paul Sartre, another famous stepfather-hater, phrased it, Pelletier had the "good grace" to die in 1941, ending a phase of unhealthy tensions. But the family stayed in Quebec City. René never returned to the Gaspé, except for a few holidays with his children and as a touring politician.

He managed to retain his position as a top mark-getter at his new school, Collège Saint-Charles-Garnier, which was also Jesuit-run. He befriended the offspring of the local bourgeoisie, young lads and lasses who were to do well in life. Among them was his wife-to-be, Louise L'Heureux, the daughter of the editor of the *Action catholique,* a newspaper much in favour with the Church, as its name suggests.

So he did adjust. But he never really liked the provincial capital. He was more at ease in bustling, multicultural Montreal. As a Liberal minister in Jean Lesage's government, he never brought more than a few changes of clothes and a shaving kit, and stayed in a tourist room near the Legislative Assembly. (Later, when he rented an apartment there, he did not even own a toaster or a coffee maker. His disdain for earthly possessions was genuine, but so was his dislike for a place he associated with loss and failure.) Strangely enough, it is in Quebec City that he is buried, in the cemetery in Sillery, alongside his mother.

Back to prewar Quebec City. When he was almost eighteen, René stopped being the model student. He began skipping classes, and did so poorly in the year-end exams that Garnier had no choice but expel him. The Séminaire de Québec was good enough to rescue him, and that is where he finished his B.A. From there he went to the faculty of law at Université Laval, where he remained an indifferent student. His interest in radio was rekindled, and he landed a part-time job as a replacement announcer with CKCV. Later, while still enrolled at Laval, he was hired full-time by Radio-Canada, the French-language network of the CBC. And there was another endeavour that kept him away from musty old law treatises for a while: theatre. In 1941 he and a friend co-authored a play, *La princesse à marier,* a comedy that lasted on the bill exactly one night, greeted as it was by hoots and boos. A monumental flop, it did not even rate a mention in his memoirs.

After two and half years of half-hearted efforts in the law faculty, René Lévesque was expelled, much to his relief and that of his professors. What to do now? The year was 1944, and for dropout students, conscription loomed.

CHAPTER FIVE

The War

To go or not to go was not at all the question for Lévesque, especially in a uniform, with a gun and a bag of rations. He was not alone in refusing to serve and could indeed find comfort in numbers. More than 80 percent of the province had voted No in the referendum on conscription in 1942. In Montreal, budding lawyer Jean Drapeau, later the city's mayor-for-life, organized demonstrations against conscription; marching with him was a student by the name of Pierre Trudeau.

There were exceptions, of course. A minority of French-speaking Quebecers did vote for conscription. One of them was a machinist living in the mill town of Shawinigan, Quebec, who went by the name of Wellie Chrétien. He reasoned that "Canada is our country, and it is at war. We must fight alongside our Allies to free Europe from the Nazi jackboot, especially France. And there is no way my boys are going to sit on their hands while lads from Ontario and Alberta are getting killed out there." His was not a popular stance, but the Chrétien boys who were fit to serve went to war, while young Trudeau studiously avoided it.

The whole matter of war and conscription affords us a glimpse into Lévesque's profoundly adolescent psychology. And here we see a less admirable trait in him: his talent for embellishment. A small example will do. René was still in Quebec City, and the war was raging in Europe. One day, accompanied by a friend, he entered a restaurant whose owner was fiddling with a shortwave radio. At one point, the voice of Hitler could be heard. The owner moved to change channels, but Lévesque stopped him. "I want to listen," he said. To the amazement of the friend, René seemed to understand everything he heard. The friend asked him where he had picked up German. "From an old priest in Gaspé," Lévesque answered. Now, there was no Germanicist at the Gaspé seminary, and Lévesque's well-researched curriculum makes no mention of any German-language course. In other words, he made it up. War would provide him opportunities galore to "adorn his autobiography," as French novelist André Malraux was fond of saying (and Malraux, being an imaginary China Hand himself, spoke as a true connoisseur).

But Lévesque was curious about the war. So he found a way out of being conscripted that came with a bonus for the cub broadcaster that he was: he applied for a job at the Montreal office of the U.S. Office of War Information and was hired, thanks mainly to his impeccable bilingualism. He would act as a translator and newsreader on the American Forces radio network. He would see the war, comment on it, but not fight in it. He would be paid a little more than $5,000 a year, a salary far superior to what his confreres in other armies were earning, and no military training was required. Not a bad deal, indeed. That said, no matter how clever his decision, the fact is that being a war correspondent is not exactly a cushy staff job; rather it is fraught with risk. So he did have courage.

What he did not always have was forthrightness. For instance, for years afterwards, he claimed to anyone who cared to listen that he had wanted to join up but did not want to wear His Majesty's uniform and get bossed around in English. And that this was why he had chosen war journalism in an American uniform. It was an explanation that certainly pleased his nationalist audience in Quebec.

The truth is that he had applied for the same kind of job at Radio-Canada but had been turned down on account of his youth and inexperience. Had he been hired, he would have had to wear the Canadian uniform he claimed to detest so much. And when Lévesque went to Korea in 1950, again as a war correspondent but this time with the CBC/Radio-Canada, he did wear the Maple Leaf–adorned uniform. Another variant of the story, again Lévesque-made: after the war, he wrote to a friend that he had packed his bag and joined up but had been seconded to the U.S. Army.

What all this demonstrates is that he was more than willing to take liberties with the truth when it suited his autobiographical profile. Also that, in his macho account tinged with guilt, he was forever seeking a moral alibi for his actions. Good training for politics.

Whatever the stories he told, his natural audience—Quebec nationalists, mainly—always believed his embellishments. As Talleyrand was fond of saying, in politics, it is what is believed that becomes the truth. That operational principle came in handy for Lévesque in later, more trying times.

On May 2, 1944, René Lévesque, then twenty-two years old, boarded a French freighter, *L'Indochinois,* en route for England.

CHAPTER SIX

Some Lessons Learned and More Tall Tales

Crossing the U-boat-infested North Atlantic, living in incessantly bombed London, seeing war-ravaged Normandy and Alsace, discovering the extermination camp at Dachau. The war was, indeed, no picnic for Lévesque. But then nor was it a tea party for the young Canadian soldiers who were killed, maimed, or taken prisoner at Dieppe and in Italy, Normandy, and Holland.

Lévesque was first sent to the U.S. Army in France in July 1944. He was later transferred to the Alsace-bound Third U.S. Army, commanded by General Patton, which was part of Omar Bradley's Twelfth U.S. Army Group. It was during the Alsace campaign that, due to acute laryngitis, he acquired the slightly husky voice that later became his signature on the waves of Radio-Canada. Finally, he was attached to General Patch's Seventh U.S. Army, fresh from Provence, where he sometimes served as liaison officer with General de Lattre de Tassigny's French forces. He entered

Germany in March 1945 and saw Dachau shortly after. The war ended on May 8, and Lévesque returned to Canada in October.

Three lessons stand out here.

Lesson one: democracy. In one of his letters home, he marvels at the sight of a "bearded Hindu" at a speakers' corner in Hyde Park castigating the decadence of the British Empire and berating the colonial yoke of India. With no one to retort that Britain was at war and that such criticism was ill-timed, the gentleman was speaking his mind freely and people listened to him calmly. It was a poignant illustration of freedom of speech that stayed with Lévesque forever.

The episode did not mark his conversion to democracy on the road to Damascus, however. Lévesque was already a visceral democrat, like all Canadians. But then Canada is a nation made up of democratic nations. From the Aboriginals, who have always been practitioners of integral democracy—whereby everybody has the right to speak up when the group has a decision to make, from the weakest to the most powerful—we borrowed the notion of "caucus" (an Algonquin word, not Latin), the weekly gathering of a party's sitting members, where the leader resumes listening to the group's suggestions and grievances in what are sometimes very robust exchanges.

The political mores of the First Nations seemed to rub off on the French settlers quickly. Under the French regime, the settlers were known for their independence of mind vis-à-vis political and administrative power. They were, as noted by the eighteenth-century writer and traveller Bougainville, "real republicans," immersed as they were in "an atmosphere of unchecked freedom." The "habitants," he observed with amazement, were totally different from their French cousins living in serfdom: they tilled vast tracts of soil, hunted and fished as they pleased, and even rode horses like noblemen in France. Bougainville added that they were, unfortunately, more than reluctant to serve the king in times of danger. Independent and free people are always like that.

Indeed, this sense of interiorized democracy is the one trait that transcends all linguistic and cultural divides in this country, and it is a reality that immigrants are quick to adjust to. Try jumping the queue anywhere in Canada or pretending that you are more equal than others, especially if you are a politician, and you'll see what I mean. Or try to snub your neighbour and see what happens next time your car gets stuck in the snow. Haughtiness in this country is simply unaffordable. Canadians are schooled in this from birth, and we probably owe our innate or acquired egalitarianism to the existential rigour of our very climate, with its biting cold in winter and clouds of mosquitoes in summer. Lévesque knew all that instinctively. The Hindu in Hyde Park simply gave a political colour to an attitude that was part and parcel of Lévesque's—and our—historical and social DNA.

Lesson two: "*les maudits Français,*" the ones in France, those goddamn Frenchmen, as they are called in Quebec, sometimes fondly, sometimes not. These are words that have crossed the lips of many self-respecting French Canadians who resent, sometimes unfairly, what is seen as an attitude of insufferable superiority. In the course of his duties, Lévesque rubbed shoulders with many Frenchmen who performed tasks similar to his, and he was quick to realize that they were no better than French Canadians, especially when it came to writing flawlessly.

He then discarded forever any sense of inferiority toward France and the French, an attitude not at all shared by his future comrades-in-arms of the Parti Québécois, most notably Jacques Parizeau and Lucien Bouchard, who thought they had reached nirvana the day they were greeted by the president of France at the Élysée palace. Not Lévesque. He could not have cared less. Moreover, what he saw in France was a vanquished population liberated in part by its dark-skinned or Arabic-speaking colonials (and by

Canadians), and a war-torn countryside, not the country of refined enlightenment that he had been taught to respect and love in his school days.

It is also in that context that Lévesque became enamoured of the all-powerful Americans. He felt more comfortable in the company of battle-dressed victors throwing chocolate bars, cigarettes, and sticks of gum to the adoring, liberated throngs than with the humbled French, especially those with a history of collaboration with the Germans.

Lesson three: Dachau. No conversion, no epiphany here, only disgust, enough of it to last a lifetime. There he saw the piled-up bodies of women, men, and children scientifically massacred or near death only because they were considered inferior to other human beings. The nationalist logic pushed to its murderous extreme.

Which raises the question: how could René Lévesque remain a nationalist after having seen Dachau first-hand? The reason is simple: he was from Quebec. Not that nationalism is worthier in Quebec; it is not. Of course, anti-Semitism afflicted it for a long time, and nationalism, in its extreme form, did exist and produced a few crackpots. But these extremists were either much derided or roundly disapproved of, and had zero credibility in any case. Lévesque had espoused, in fact, minority nationalism, a school of thought that is very different from majority nationalism. Whereas the latter tends to be exclusionary, intolerant of dissent and foreignness, sometimes murderous in its tribalism, minority nationalism tends to be more positive. It focuses on equality of rights and conditions of existence; it is capable of embracing modernity, moderation, tolerance, diversity. But it is not without flaws: its emphasis on particularism to the detriment of universal values, its tendency to look inward instead of taking a global view, its glorification of grievances, real or imagined. Especially imagined.

In Dachau, Lévesque saw with his own eyes what unbridled nationalism could do, and that instilled in him a lasting skepticism about any expression of fanaticism. Lévesque might have learned a similar lesson from witnessing Benito Mussolini's hanging and the arrest of Field Marshal Hermann Göring—if he had been there to witness them, that is. But he was not there, even though he told the tale as if he had been. Now, Lévesque as a politician was not one to lie for political advantage. But when it came to his war exploits, he succumbed to the temptation of self-aggrandizement. The motivation here lies simply in his juvenile desire to charm an audience; he just could not help himself. You would have thought, though, that the aging process would have tempered that tendency in him. It did not.

Lévesque was able to get away with his exaggerations for much of his life. The furor erupted only when he published his memoirs, in 1986. In the first edition of his *Memoirs,* he was foolish enough to include not one but two fabrications. The first was his much-vaunted account of the lynching of Benito Mussolini and his mistress, Clara Petacci, near Milan. He had earlier described to an interviewer the blood dripping from the human slabs of meat, the revulsion he had felt. On that day, however, Lévesque had been with Patch's army in Munich. And the second was how he had witnessed the arrest of Göring. The arrest was dramatic from his point of view, but it had been told to him. He had arrived, in fact, fifteen minutes too late. Although most readers apparently did not mind, as evidenced by the healthy sales of his memoirs, better-informed journalists took him to task for his embellishments. He had to backtrack but did so only very reluctantly.

CHAPTER SEVEN

The Good Years …
Under Duplessis

In November 1945, barely a month after returning home, René Lévesque was hired as an announcer at La Voix du Canada, Radio-Canada's international service. He had a cushy job, a steady salary, and he was living the good life in Montreal, far enough from parochial Quebec City.

In 1947 he married his very patient sweetheart from Quebec City, Louise L'Heureux. Children soon followed: Pierre in 1948, Claude in 1950, Suzanne in 1956. Lévesque eventually bought a home and, like everyone else, led a life similar to the one portrayed in the popular TV show *Father Knows Best:* he went to work in the morning and came home at night and read the paper while his wife made dinner and the children played in the backyard.

Life was good for other Quebecers, too. They were leaving the countryside in droves to find work in the cities. The post-war economy was booming, and people were enthusiastically getting acquainted with the electrical appliances and other conveniences that made life so much better. They no longer had to fetch water from the well, so the morning shower slowly replaced the Saturday-night bath. The suburbs around Montreal were exploding, as were car sales. The Catholic Church was as powerful as ever, and order reigned under the tight-fisted premier-for-life Maurice Duplessis.

But life was not so good if you were a political dissenter like Pierre Trudeau, whose appointment to the law faculty of the University of Montreal was blocked for a long time because he was suspected of communist leanings. It was even worse if you were a Jehovah's Witness. Duplessis relentlessly persecuted the Witnesses, with the blessing of the Church and without a peep from French-speaking intellectuals.

Life was not too promising either if you dreamed of a good education. Imbued with a conservative, paternalistic outlook on life, Duplessis believed that children belonged to parents and that the government had no right to force them to attend high school or any institution of higher learning. That was one of the reasons why he turned down federal subsidies to Quebec universities, a move he defended by invoking provincial jurisdiction over education.

It was also a bad time for the unionized workers of the province, whose strikes for better working conditions were routinely declared illegal. Most noteworthy here was the

February 1949 strike in the Asbestos and Thetford mines. Five thousand workers walked out on their employer, the Johns-Manville Corporation, after negotiations had failed. They wanted the company to protect both towns from asbestos dust; they demanded a fifteen-cent increase in the hourly wage, plus an extra five cents an hour for the night shift; and they asked for the implementation of the Rand formula (where employees within a bargaining unit must pay union dues, but actual membership in the union is voluntary). Premier Duplessis sided immediately with the company and sent in his Quebec Provincial Police (QPP) to guard the mines and protect the scabs. On May 6, after a few violent incidents pitting strikers against scabs, the Riot Act was read and the QPP arrested hundreds of strikers, beating a good number of them senseless. The strike ended in June, with very few gains for the workers.

The Asbestos Strike was not the watershed moment that some later claimed it was. But it did leave some scars on Quebec society. Duplessis and Johns-Manville had had the upper hand, but the Church came out of it somewhat weakened. Some members of the clergy had supported the company, but many more had thrown in their lot with the workers. The Archbishop of Montreal, Joseph Charbonneau, had expressed his support for the workers, which infuriated Duplessis. Charbonneau was soon transferred to Victoria, never to be seen again in the province of Quebec. From then on, the Church began losing its grip over Catholic workers' unions. Things would never be the same again, although no one knew it at the time.

The strike also allowed three young intellectuals to earn their stripes in the public domain. The most visible one was Jean Marchand, the young labour leader who spearheaded the workers' struggle. The second one was a former Catholic activist who had become a first-rate journalist at *Le Devoir,* Gérard Pelletier. He spent many months in the strikers' towns at a time when most news outlets were almost silent on the strike for fear of displeasing Duplessis. Pelletier and Marchand were living more or less in a war zone, and their involvement required real physical courage. The third one was labour lawyer Pierre Trudeau, who was to become the heart and soul of a small but epoch-making periodical called *Cité Libre.* His support for the strike was unequivocal, a stance that required courage as well, but he was not as involved as Pelletier and Marchand. Seventeen years later, the three would team up again to go to Ottawa and try to change the country, which they did.

Now, if you were an artist in the Duplessis era, life could be downright miserable. Duplessis contemptuously referred to artists as "piano players." On August 9, 1948, a group of young painters and poets calling themselves the automatists published a manifesto entitled *Refus global,* in which they called for an end to moral dictatorship over art. Some of its signatories were harshly punished. Painter Paul-Émile Borduas was fired from the École du meuble, where he taught. Some, like painter Jean-Paul Riopelle, moved to France, where his career flourished. Others, like painter Marcelle Ferron and playwright and poet Claude Gauvreau, who had penned the manifesto, pursued their work here and abroad but did so in total obscurity for a very long time. Today, the signatories of *Refus global* have all been rehabilitated in the public memory; they are hailed as courageous pioneers; there is even a federal riding named after Borduas.

In 1952 the screening of Marcel Carné's epic film *Les Enfants du Paradis,* based on Jacques Prévert's screenplay and featuring luminaries of the French cinema such as Arletty and Jean-Louis Barrault, was banned by Quebec government censors. You still had to ask permission from your bishop to read sulphurous authors such as Victor Hugo, Baudelaire, or Rimbaud.

There were exceptions. In Montreal, you could easily find such authors and even works by Sartre and Jean Genet in English-owned bookstores that had enough business savvy to cater to a famished French readership. And artists of the *Refus global* mould could hang their artwork in Jewish-owned galleries. But you could not stage a Bertolt Brecht play. And any artistic depiction of sex remained verboten.

However, it was because of this moral order that the Duplessis years are rightly remembered as a detestable time by just about everybody. French-speaking Quebecers had been living in the shadow of the Church forever, but the 1950s were a time of unchallenged moral serfdom: you existed officially only after baptism; in your school years, you were likely to have as a teacher a cornet-wearing nun or a cassocked brother who would spend an inordinate amount of time drilling catechism into you. Mass, said in Latin, was packed on Sundays, and you were encouraged to go to church every morning if you had the time for it. The whole year was punctuated by religious events: the Immaculate Conception, Advent, Christmas, Lent, Easter, Pentecost, you name it. And there were the rites of First Communion and Confirmation to mark your passage through life, not to mention regular confession, during which the priest would suggest to Madame So-and-so that six children was a nice start for a family. Abortion and divorce were dirty words no one dared to utter. Then there were the vespers, meatless

Fridays, a thousand religious organizations you would be strongly invited to join, from the Brownies and Cubs all the way to the Daughters of Isabella and the Knights of Columbus. You would enter adulthood and get married in church, your children would be baptized, and the whole cycle would start all over again. You would die in the arms of the Church, with a priest administering extreme unction. There was just no escape. When passing by a church, it was not unusual for bus drivers to remove their caps and for the more dutiful riders to make the sign of the cross. Anyone undertaking a lengthy car trip would start out by reciting a couple of Hail Marys and the Our Father for good luck. My personal favourite was the local bishop reciting the rosary on the radio at 7 P.M. every day: a real thrill.

Now those were exceptionally "moral" times elsewhere too, in McCarthyist America, for example. (Post-Edwardian anglophone Canada was a bit better, but perhaps mainly because there was no dominant church.) Quebecers were thus not alone in chafing under such strict rules. But one who was not chafing at all was René Lévesque. He lived well, travelled at public expense, and had love affairs galore while his wife raised the kids, cooked, and ironed. As an up-and-coming broadcasting star, he enjoyed all the pleasures reserved for the happy few and forbidden to the unhappy masses. He behaved as if the sheer unfairness of widespread moral servitude legitimized all transgressions.

His career took off, too. He blossomed as an announcer and was soon assigned to reporting, moving from the international service to the national network. Then came the war in Korea, for which he volunteered as a correspondent in 1950. That experience established for good his credentials as a serious journalist. He was supposed to stay there for six months, but his wife had him recalled after three. He then was rewarded with many prestigious assignments, for instance, covering the visit to Canada of French president Vincent Auriol in 1951 and the American presidential elections in 1952. He also moonlighted as a movie reviewer for various newspapers and magazines. In short, his name was almost made.

And then came TV.

CHAPTER EIGHT

Stardom

Like most other Canadians, Quebecers had fallen in love with television. So overwhelming was the *coup de foudre* that although in some regions near the U.S. border only American broadcasts would come in, unilingual French Quebecers lapped it up anyway. Kids could be seen in the streets of small towns re-enacting their favourite show, *The Adventures of Kit Carson,* speaking in a made-up mumbo-jumbo language they believed was English. That was how it sounded to them anyway.

By the mid-1950s, four out of five households in the province had a television set. And when the French-speaking people of Canada were all able to view locally made, francophone productions, they became a tight-knit virtual family, discussing at length the ending of the last sitcom or drama millions of others had watched, adopting as their own actors and actresses they had grown fond of, or, conversely, expressing unanimous hate for TV villains like Séraphin, the miser in the seemingly endless *Les Belles Histoires des Pays d'En-Haut,* which everybody watched. For good reason, too:

there was only one French-language TV station; Radio-Canada's monopoly ensured that all, and I mean all, francophones growing up in Quebec in the 1950s and 1960s shared a single TV culture.

Lévesque was a regular commentator on current events programs, but he was mainly heard on the radio—until someone at Radio-Canada had the good sense to give him his own show in October 1957.

Here begins the legend of René Lévesque.

The show was called *Point de mire* (Focal Point), a thirty-minute live broadcast first airing on Sundays at 11:15 P.M. and later, due to the show's growing popularity, on Tuesdays at 10:30 P.M. For many, it was another *coup de foudre*. Here was this little man with the funny voice, equipped with a blackboard, a pointer, and maps, explaining the outside world to French-speaking Canadians, talking very fast but using only intelligible words. Let me paraphrase him: "Good evening. Thank you for joining me. Tonight, we are off to the Suez. It's in Egypt, the land of the pharaohs that became mummies, you know, the land of the pyramids and the Sphinx. Here on the map is a canal, called Suez, built by French and British engineers in the last century. You can see here that it links up the Mediterranean and the Red Sea. So a very important route for international trade, because, thanks to the canal, ships stopped having to go all around the African continent to take their goods to the Orient, or the other way around. See?" (And he would circle Africa with his pointer.) "Without Suez, the cup of tea from India you just had would cost you more because it would have to travel much farther. You follow me? Now, the Egyptians no longer have pharaohs. Egypt is now a republic, led by a man they call the Raïs—which means 'president' in Arabic—a man by the name of Nasser. So ..." And on he would go. For many Quebecers with little schooling, *Point de mire* became their first window on the world. Not everybody watched, of course, but those who did were enthralled, especially news junkies and all those hungry for knowledge. And in Duplessis's Quebec, there were a lot of them. Thanks to the Radio-Canada monopoly, Lévesque's ratings sometimes reached 100 percent: a dream for any broadcaster and now an impossible feat, even on days such as September 11, 2001.

To take the helm of *Point de mire*, Lévesque had had to give up his comfortable job as a broadcaster, with the guaranteed income, pension, and other benefits. But he was now earning $20,000 a year—more than any Cabinet minister, provincial or federal. The real payoff, however, was instant celebrity. René Lévesque was now the star journalist who could explain the school desegregation in Little Rock, Arkansas; the violent decolonization of Algeria; or the partition of Berlin and Cyprus. He could not walk the streets of Quebec without being accosted by adoring fans who would stop him to shake his hand and thank him. All of a sudden, he had become "Monsieur Lévesque." And he was more than loved; he was respected. In the words of novelist and social commentator Jacques Godbout, Lévesque was Quebec's "first lay teacher."

Of course, the viewers did not see the man who never read his fan mail and never returned phone calls. Undisciplined but hard-working, incessantly feasting on magazines and newspapers in his smoke-filled office or at McGill's nearby library to prepare for his weekly rendezvous with live television. Stressed out, as we would say today, but always focused. The badly dressed and unsuspected Lothario with doubtful hygiene who ate, talked, and smoked all at once, leaving a mess behind him all the time, driving like a madman in the streets in Montreal. Famous for his all-night poker-playing, his chain-smoking; fond of sleeping late and seldom on time for appointments. Never at home, never where he was supposed to be. It was as though he was living three lives at the same time.

It was also during those years that he met Pierre Trudeau. The meeting took place in the Radio-Canada cafeteria, where artists and journalists congregated between assignments to talk and reshape the world in keeping with the fantasies and ideals in vogue. Trudeau was then a law professor and sometime TV commentator known for his scathing wit and erudition. He was well travelled, one of the few men in Canada who had visited China and reported on it. His *Cité Libre* was one of the very rare publications that dared to criticize Duplessis and public policy. Its circulation was of confidential proportions, but it was influential within the small, thinking elite of the era.

The person who introduced them was journalist Gérard Pelletier, who was a friend of both Trudeau and Lévesque. For once, as Pelletier said later, Lévesque was not running, slowed down by the overflowing cup of coffee in his one hand and the stack of newspapers under his other arm. Pelletier motioned to him to come and sit down with him and the slightly balding man with the piercing blue eyes. He had wanted the two to meet for a long time. For the occasion, Trudeau put on his best snotty-nosed behaviour, complete with the French mid-Atlantic accent he had acquired at Montreal's Jesuit-run Brébeuf College. Lévesque played the nonchalant TV star. This is how Pelletier remembers their conversation. I've added what I imagine must have been their internal dialogue in square brackets.

Trudeau: Ah, the famous René Lévesque! How do you do? [Your *Point de mire* celebrity does not impress me at all, you should know that.] You speak well, sir, very well, but tell me something: can you write, too?

Lévesque: Yes, but you know, writing takes time … [Don't even think for a minute I would waste a second reading your *Cité Libre* …]

Trudeau: Yes, you are right. You need time, and you also need to have ideas of your own, things to say, you know … [Watch out, buddy, I bite too.]

The two were chalk and cheese from the get-go. They would meet again.

CHAPTER NINE

The Epiphany: Variations on a Theme

The dream world of *Point de mire* soon came to an abrupt halt. When Lévesque walked into the office on December 29, 1958, his secretary told him that Radio-Canada producers had gone on strike. He had only one comment: "Bunch of losers!" Of course, he was protected by his iron-clad contract, so the money would keep flowing in, but his voice would be heard no more, and his face would disappear from the tube.

The association representing the seventy-four Radio-Canada producers had been negotiating with the top brass for a while, and talks had failed. The producers were considered management by the corporation and paid accordingly, but they could also be displaced or removed in an instant; they were at the mercy of the wishes and whims of the corporation. Now the producers wanted to be acknowledged as a bargaining unit in order to negotiate better working conditions, such as employment security, benefits, and pensions. The corporation retorted that such a move would hamper management's flexibility and stifle the producers' creativity.

Lévesque soon forgot his knee-jerk comment. He was quickly engulfed in the strike, as were the hundreds of other craftspeople of the corporation who refused to cross the picket lines. In short order, he enthusiastically joined the strikers and their sympathizers at nightly satirical shows they put on in order to build their strike fund. He also contributed to their publication, *Difficultés temporaires* (Temporary Interference), and wrote eloquent op-ed pieces in mainstream newspapers explaining the strikers' cause.

In today's Quebec the Radio-Canada producers' strike enjoys the same mythical status as the *Refus global* manifesto of 1948 and the subsequent hounding of its signatories and the Asbestos Strike (where Prime Minister Lester Pearson's three wise men to be—Marchand, Pelletier, and Trudeau— had cut their teeth). But the producers' strike was largely an elitist affair, the strikers being, after all, well-paid white-collar workers of the chattering class. As for the general public, who were deprived of their usual programming, they were treated to movies from dawn till dusk for the sixty-eight days that the strike lasted: the film-fest of the century. Few complained.

After a while, because Radio-Canada was a federal institution, the strikers took their dispute to Ottawa. Off they went, by train, to meet the labour minister in John Diefenbaker's Progressive Conservative government, Michael Starr. The good minister, who did not speak a word of French but had been well briefed, agreed to meet with the strikers. His sole answer was that, since Radio-Canada—the CBC—was an arm's-length corporation, there was nothing he could do. Sorry. The strikers went home empty-handed.

For Lévesque, that moment was his epiphany. As he recounted later, "If CBC producers had gone on strike in Toronto, Parliament would have acted without delay so as to not disrupt programming for the English-speaking public." (And, he might have added, to protect the CBC from American and private competition.) "The matter would have been resolved in a few days. But since there were only French viewers involved, they couldn't care less." Two solitudes, he felt, one less equal than the other. For years he would claim that never before had he felt like a second-class citizen in the country of his birth. In other words, the Radio-Canada strike was to Lévesque a *Refus global* and Asbestos Strike rolled into one, the difference being that the enemy here was not an authoritarian Quebec but an English Canada too distant for his taste.

Lévesque was accompanied to the meeting in Ottawa by labour leader Jean Marchand, later a federal minister, and Jean-Louis Roux, a then-well-known actor who would one day be appointed to the Senate and also become Lieutenant-Governor of Quebec. Marchand and Roux did not share Lévesque's resentment toward the federal government. Lévesque may have been right about Ottawa's indifference to French Canada over the producers' strike, but why did it estrange him from his country to such a degree? Simply put, the disaffection he was feeling was looking for a political home. A common phenomenon in the Canadian political periphery at all times, in the case of Quebec, disaffection was—and still is—exacerbated by the language difference and the calluses and bruises of memory.

It must also be pointed out that, in those days, Lévesque's feelings were echoed by many young academics and intellectuals from Quebec, who, unable to find work under Duplessis, had found refuge in the federal civil service and discovered that their cultural identity was something best checked at the door when they went to work. Officers in the Canadian Forces and the Royal Canadian Mounted Police were pointedly told not to speak French, even among themselves. But it was something that was never discussed; people just dealt with it, in silence, as obedient Catholics were wont to do in those days.

If the producers' strike coalesced Lévesque's feeling of rejection by Canada, it was only a seed clamouring for more water. He and many of his contemporaries were already souring on the then-dominant strain of French-Canadian nationalism that was, well, French Canadian, not yet "Québécois." It was largely a lyrical and mystical discourse based on the celebration of a Great All-Catholic French Canada, the manifest destiny of which was to civilize first a savage America and then an Anglo-Protestant and capitalist America. It exalted in the sufferings of the deported Acadians, the fate of the French-speaking Métis after the legalized murder of Louis Riel, the long-drawn-out battles for French schools in Ontario and Manitoba. It was a world where the preferred heroes were victims of the Iroquois or the English. But it was essentially a Church-inspired ideology whose propagandists had been avowed admirers of now-discredited figures such as Pétain, Franco, and Mussolini. Religious estrangement, although an underground and largely urban phenomenon at the time, had already begun. Political alienation would soon follow.

We know, in retrospect, but even at the time, that for Lévesque and many others of his generation that brand of French-Catholic nationalism was already old hat and utopic, and they were slowly beginning to believe that the fate of

North American French-speakers lay in Quebec, nowhere else. In fact, Lévesque was never kind to his self-exiled brethren, whom he considered to be hopelessly assimilated, even dismissing them as "dead ducks" at one point. Thus, in a way, he did not suffer much in his feeling of exclusion from Canada. Psychologically, he was more inclined to pack his bags and retreat to more hospitable ground, where he could at least be master of his domain. For many like him, it was more and more a conscious and viable political choice.

One final comment about the Radio-Canada strike: Lévesque had acquired new tastes in that battle. He had taken to the streets with the strikers and had even been arrested by the police in the course of a demonstration (only to be released a couple of hours later); he had been applauded on stage night after night as a leader; his views had been sought; he had been listened to, and this time not as a journalist. He had partaken in the melee with glee and speculated on the politics of the whole issue with some flair.

Politics ...

CHAPTER TEN

The Honest Wrestler

The broadcaster as politician. A Canadian phenomenon? The word *Canada* means "village" in the Iroquoian language, and since journalists gain notoriety easily in our often small-town context, the move from the microphone or the pen to the hustings is an easy one. Indeed, a seemingly inordinate number of journalists end up in politics, although they are less well represented in the legislatures than farmers and certainly lawyers. Some of them even do well: Brian Tobin and Sheila Copps come to mind. Among the very successful, three names stand out: radio preacher "Bible Bill" Aberhart, who became premier of Alberta in the 1930s, Joey Smallwood of Newfoundland, and René Lévesque. While he was in politics, Lévesque had to contend with rivals who came from the same line of work as he, namely *Cité Libre*'s Pierre Trudeau and *Le Devoir*'s Claude Ryan. Apparently journalists are tempted by politics as much as politicians are attracted to journalists.

Lévesque benefited from that attraction. In 1960, as a provincial election was looming in Quebec, he and various other media figures—including Gérard Pelletier and Trudeau—were courted by Liberals banking on their name recognition. After the Radio-Canada strike, Lévesque's contract had not been renewed. He had gone to private radio in 1959, but his heart was no longer in it. He was a public man in search of a new audience, so he heeded the Liberals' call. He soon was slated as their candidate in the Montreal riding of Laurier.

It was an audacious career move, since success was far from a foregone conclusion. The then-ruling Union Nationale (UN) had money to spare, knew the terrain extremely well, and had the incumbency advantage. But they had two problems. One was their leader. Duplessis had died in September 1959 and been replaced by Paul Sauvé, whose slogan, "Désormais" (From Now On), inaugurated what became known as the Quiet Revolution. Under his watch, Quebec had finally agreed to federal subsidies for universities. It was an auspicious start. But Sauvé had died a few months later, and his successor was a bland nobody by the name of Antonio Barrette. His vis-à-vis was youngish, TV-friendly Jean Lesage, a former Liberal minister in Ottawa under Louis St-Laurent who had had enough of languishing in an Official Opposition seemingly unable to topple John Diefenbaker's Progressive Conservatives. That was precisely the UN's other problem: the presence in Ottawa of another Conservative government.

Canadians seem to vote wisely. Every time they hand the levers of power in the provincial capital to a conservative party, they put the federal government in the hands of a party with progressive views. This is how they balance their own natural resistance to shaking things up with the need for change that animates any dynamic, modern society. For instance, in the Trudeau years, which were marked by revolutionary changes on a Canadian scale—think of coast-to-coast bilingualism and the move to the metric system—Ontario entrusted the power at Queen's Park to the wilfully bland but efficient Tories. With Trudeau gone and the Conservative Mulroney comfortably in charge of Ottawa, Ontarians elected Liberal David Peterson to Queen's Park, and then went even further left by voting in Bob Rae's New Democratic Party a few years later.

Examples of these checks and balances abound in the federation, but Quebecers play the game admirably well. They have rarely had parties of the same colour in power in both Ottawa and Quebec City, and much to their benefit, as it turned out. From 1935 to 1957, Quebecers kept Liberals Mackenzie King and Louis St-Laurent in Ottawa; both favoured moderate but necessary social measures, such as unemployment insurance, family allowances, and old age pensions. At the same time, they brought to power Maurice Duplessis's UN in Quebec City; Duplessis was fiercely right wing and hostile to change in just about every domain.

Quebecers thus reconciled the two political tendencies harboured by every other Canadian: resistance and change. And that is how they ended up pocketing allowances and pensions from Ottawa while satisfying their appetite for moral order.

Their wiliness reached a new height in the Trudeau era, when they elected René Lévesque's Parti Québécois in Quebec City, thus opposing federalist to secessionist in a contest that the original democrats, the Athenians, would have applauded for its wisdom. In a federation such as Canada, this conferring of control to opposite political tendencies at various levels of power allows voters to find balance—as well as entertainment worthy of the best theatre. Not that every Canadian voter is an armchair strategist, thinking, I just voted for a Conservative in Halifax, who got elected, and now, to keep him honest, I am going to vote for a Liberal in Ottawa. Few people are that Machiavellian.

The members of any federation, however united they may be by their common interest, remain natural rivals, especially in the domains of shared jurisdiction (environment and agriculture). That is why the provinces regularly gang up on Ottawa between elections and why the federal government has a vested interest in posing as the champion of all Canadians. They both have to please the same voters. And the voter, having the luxury to vote at different intervals in our political system, always profits from the affection showered on him or her by the two contenders.

Voters do sometimes send rulers to both the provincial and the federal capital who have the same ideology. During the Second World War, for example, Quebecers put Liberals in power in both Quebec City and Ottawa. And in Alberta, in the 1930s, voters dispatched Calgary Conservative R.B. Bennett as prime minister to Ottawa and later elected the even more right-wing Social Crediter Bill Aberhart in Edmonton. However, political kinship does not guarantee harmony. Remember: it is politicians who are elected, and self-interest is always sure to trump ideology. So when Bennett created the Bank of Canada to foster monetary stability in a country where banks until then printed their own currency, in order to restore public confidence in the Canadian dollar, he had to butt heads with Alberta's Aberhart, who wanted to create his own bank, in keeping with Social Credit orthodoxy. Bennett won that battle, and his party paid dearly for it in Alberta. The only ones to benefit from the squabble were the Alberta voters, who were rewarded with a safe dollar and retained in their provincial legislature a party that was as moral in its outlook as Duplessis's UN. Did the Alberta voters plan it that way? I doubt it, but the result was enviable nonetheless.

Such were the waters into which René Lévesque was about to plunge. Lesage not only had the good fortune of having a Conservative government in Ottawa; he was also surrounded by new faces, people who promised change, worthy and sophisticated men most of them. He called them "*l'équipe du tonnerre*" (the dream team). But he knew that wresting power from the UN would not be easy.

IN THE RIDING OF LAURIER, Lévesque was facing Arsène Gagné, an old-school ward heeler at the head of a well-oiled political machine that resorted to every trick in the book to beat the Liberal newcomer. They ranged from accusing Lévesque of communist sympathies to running a candidate whose name was also René Lévesque in order to confuse voters. The UN also practised physical intimidation. But in this case, Gagné's thugs tried to intimidate the wrong man. He was Jean "Johnny" Rougeau, a resident of the riding and a famous wrestler. Not only was Rougeau unimpressed, he even reacted by volunteering as René Lévesque's chauffeur and bodyguard. Lévesque was grateful, as times were tough for challengers in those days.

Chapter One of René Lévesque's political legend: "So disgusted were the voters by the corrupt practices of the UN that they suddenly longed for an honest figure to represent them. And the man chosen by the Liberals to run in Laurier was so clean that he even attracted the support of Johnny Rougeau, the honest wrestler whose bouts were never fixed, never ..." Well, so says the legend.

The truth was a little different. As Liberal organizers later admitted, they, too, had to cut some corners to get Lévesque elected. Everybody was cheating, they said, so you were forced to bend the rules too. Lévesque himself had to throw aside his mistress, who was the mother of his illegitimate daughter, and reconcile with his wife, and do it fast, for Lesage did not want any of his candidates to be separated or divorced. Louise Lévesque was good enough to take René back.

On June 22, 1960, Lévesque squeaked in by a mere 129 votes. He was not alone in winning by a slight margin. As Graham Fraser shows in his still very relevant *PQ: René Lévesque and the Parti Québécois in Power,* it had been very close in several ridings. Paul Gérin-Lajoie, another star contestant, had a majority of only 149 votes. As Fraser points out, if 400 Quebecers had voted the other way, the Quiet Revolution would have been postponed by another four years. The Liberals had garnered 51 percent of the popular vote to the UN's 47 percent, which translated into fifty seats for Lesage and forty-four for his UN opponent, who was soon gone and forgotten. The razor-thin victory suggested that Quebec was ready for a change, yes, but that resistance to it was also very strong.

Indeed, the Catholic, Duplessis brand of Quebec conservatism was still very much alive. Two years later, at the federal level, the colourful Réal Caouette and his Social Credit, a party enamoured of the most archaic and right-wing ideas, elected twenty-six members. Resistance to change had only changed addresses. That's Canadian voters from coast to coast: whenever they dismiss traditional parties such as the Liberals and the Conservatives as tired and corrupt or not right wing enough, they flock to new parties with old ideas. To wit, Preston Manning's Reform, Lucien Bouchard's Bloc Québécois, and Mario Dumont's Action démocratique du Québec.

CHAPTER ELEVEN

"Oui, Monsieur le Ministre"

Lévesque was made minister of hydroelectric resources and public works, and he wasted no time imposing his style. In this portfolio, he instituted the practice of calling for tenders for any government contract over $25,000. No longer were the friends of the party in power automatically favoured for lucrative public works contracts, as had been the way under the Union Nationale. Under the UN, if you were a friend of the party and donated generously to the right bagmen, miracles happened, and everlasting happiness was guaranteed for all.

Chapter Two of Lévesque's political legend: he turned down the fat envelopes of bills handed to him early in his tenure, and he made it clear to his staff that no one was to benefit illicitly from their closeness to power. Some of his colleagues in caucus and Cabinet began to grumble: Why, since our own moneymen did so much to rid us of the UN's corrupt ways, couldn't you show some gratitude to those who helped us out in the past? I mean, what is this holier-than-thou attitude? Come on, René ... Lévesque was, in fact, powerless to change the shady practices of the times, but he had launched a trend he would pick up later.

In the spring of 1961 Lesage then found him a cause worthier of his reform-minded zeal. Lévesque was relieved of public works and handed the new Natural Resources Ministry, which combined two portfolios, mines and hydro-electric resources.

Lévesque's new domain was ideally suited to him. Public ownership of the province's natural resources, especially hydroelectric power, was already an old hobby horse for Quebec nationalists. They had campaigned hard for it in the 1930s, and the Liberal leader Adélard Godbout had heeded their call when he became premier in 1939 with the creation of Hydro-Québec. Its purview was, however, limited to the island of Montreal, and after Duplessis had regained power in 1944, he made sure that the rest of the province belonged to private companies and co-operatives. Nevertheless, Hydro-Québec was big business, with assets of more than $1 billion and $100 million a year in revenue. The rest of the power grid was a patchwork shared by big corporations such as Shawinigan Heat & Power Ltd., more modest but also very profitable family-owned companies, and some forty electrical co-ops. But it was like the Wild West. There was little regulation. Private companies charged what they wanted. Distribution was uneven and the voltage varied from one region to another, with dire consequences for the supply of households and businesses. In some places, you could have two different systems side by side. Service was very inadequate in frontier regions such as Abitibi. In the Gaspé Peninsula, hydro cost six times as much as in Quebec City. Another problem for Quebec nationalists: technicians and managers were trained and worked mostly in English. In short, the target was irresistible for a minister with nationalist convictions and the will to modernize the system for the benefit of the entire population of Quebec.

As soon as Lévesque had a clear idea of the situation, he entrusted the whole operation to a young economist by the name of Jacques Parizeau. The plan was to use Hydro-Québec as a basis for buying out or expropriating all other companies. They would need to borrow money for that, a lot of it. The main problem here was not Hydro-Québec's credit but the financial syndicate of Ames & Co. of Montreal, which held a virtual monopoly on all the loans to the Government of Quebec. To Lévesque and Parizeau, the fellows at the helm of Ames & Co. must have seemed to come straight out of a comic strip—big, muscular Anglo capitalists as they had always imagined them: Scotch-drinking and cigar-chomping, treating the Quebec government as a cash cow of their own, with only contempt for those French-speaking politicians foolish enough to run for office, where no money was to be made, and whose dreams were too big for their small brains.

So the Parizeau team did what no one could have imagined doing in Quebec before: they bypassed Ames & Co. and went knocking on other doors. They ended up in New York City, where the financiers looked at the deal and said, "This looks promising. How much do you need?" Parizeau was flabbergasted: it had been as easy as pie. For young men like him, not used to big money and to dealing with total strangers on Wall Street, the whole operation was a confidence-building exercise whose lesson would not be lost on a new class of Quebec technocrats with ambition to spare.

The minister of natural resources now had to secure the support of Lesage and his Cabinet. The big decision was made at a special Cabinet meeting at Lac-à-l'épaule, a government-owned resort. There was a lot of hemming and hawing. The very concept of state-owned electricity was repugnant to some ministers. It smacked of socialism—How will the business community react? What will the very conservative people of Quebec say?—but Lévesque was well prepared. He pointed out that Ontario had gone through exactly the same operation in 1906 without anyone complaining, then or since. British Columbia had done it as recently as 1961. Manitoba, even little New Brunswick had done it. More importantly, as Lévesque patiently explained, the Quebec government could afford it. The argument that won the day belonged to Georges-Émile Lapalme, the bright and respected former Liberal leader and minister of cultural affairs, who reminded everyone present that Lévesque's project had been a long-standing Liberal promise. Lesage then decreed that he had a consensus: he would support the idea and it would become the central theme of the next general election. "Anything else? Gentlemen, thank you." That was it. Lévesque had won a very important political battle. The Liberals now had to convince the voters.

The nationalization of electricity became the talk of the town in the November 1962 general election. It dwarfed the other accomplishments of the Liberal administration, namely, the creation of a system of health insurance and the reinstatement of compulsory education, with free schooling from kindergarten to high school, in a province where, thanks to Duplessis's outmoded concepts, four out of five Quebecers had not gone beyond elementary school. The Liberals' slogan was *Maîtres chez nous* (Masters in Our Own

House), the nationalist war cry of the 1930s that had been the brainchild of none other than Lionel Groulx. It was a classic case of political poaching on the UN's territory, but it worked.

Front and centre in the campaign was René Lévesque, of course. His impassioned pleas made him into a political star. He criss-crossed the province with his *Point de mire* blackboard and pointer, explaining to everyone the advantages of owning the power produced by Quebec's own rivers. Audiences loved it.

The whole matter of nationalization was a curious blend of economic common sense and emotion. At the time, not many Quebecers owned their own home. Sure, if you were a habitant operating a farm and were the first-born of the family, you could hope to own your father's land one day. But if you were an unschooled worker toiling in a town or city, chances were slim that you would ever own the ground under your feet. The vast majority of French-speaking people living in the towns and cities of the province rented their homes, at a time when only homeowners had the right to vote in municipal elections (a practice inherited from the old French regime of the *seigneurs*). This meant that renters were totally disenfranchised when it came to decisions regarding traffic lights, sewers, parks, whatever. In Montreal,

English-speaking citizens were more likely to own their homes than francophones, so who made the big decisions in Montreal? The English-speakers, of course. The average Québécois was paying rent in the province he thought he owned. What is more, this undemocratic system dragged on for another decade. The Liberal government of Robert Bourassa changed the law in 1971, and renters finally got the right to vote in municipal elections.

The public appropriation of electricity thus seemed like compensation in the minds of many voters, their reasoning going along these lines: "I may have nothing and own nothing, but this hydro business is going to be ours. I will become an owner after all." "Exactly my point," Lévesque would say. "And think of the contagious effect this collective decision could have: one day, we could also own our mines, our forests, our fisheries, everything that's rightfully ours. People will be collective owners and shareholders. What else will you be tempted to own? Your own home, your own business? Come on, let's go for it!" The crowds would roar their approval. He would go on: "Not only that: the companies that now take our electricity and sell it to us at high prices will be replaced by your company, Hydro-Québec. We, and nobody else, will make our own decisions, right here. And now think of all those engineers, technicians, and managers who will now be trained in French and will work in French!" The crowds would be delirious. Lévesque's magic words would touch everybody profoundly.

The Liberals were re-elected with a bigger majority, in large part thanks to René Lévesque.

CHAPTER TWELVE

Him Again

Yes, him: Pierre Trudeau. What was he up to in those heady years? The usual: teaching law, travelling, writing. Also honing his skills in the big debate of the time in Quebec: the place of French Canadians in the federation.

He and Lévesque would sometimes meet at André Laurendeau's Outremont home. Laurendeau was not so much a mentor or father figure to them, but more a wise old friend they both liked and admired. A man with an aristo-cratic bearing and a pen to match, sporting a pencil-thin moustache à la Clark Gable. Known for his moderate views, he exerted a great deal of influence as the respected editor of *Le Devoir*. Often torn between Quebec and Canada, he had strong reservations about Quebec independence and equally strong doubts about Canada's tolerance of the French fact. He is remembered today for having said that "any self-respecting Quebecer is a separatist at least an hour a day," a phrase that expresses the ambivalence of many Quebecers toward Canada. Trudeau, Lévesque, journalist Gérard Pelletier, and labour organizer Jean Marchand would often join him in his salon to discuss current events and the future of Quebec.

Trudeau had no time for Lévesque's economic nationalism and Hydro-Québec. He felt that French Canadians should engage in a sort of repossession of the country that was rightfully theirs. He excoriated Quebec intellectuals who refused to leave the province and fight for their rights; he felt asphyxiated in a province that refused to think beyond its borders; and he believed in his bones that all French Canadians had to do was show their English counterparts that they were as good as them. Excellence was the way of the future, and if we Quebecers succeed, he wrote, the French language will become a "status symbol" everywhere in Canada and will never again be a language spoken by some inferior tribe. Most of these views had been expounded in his famous *Cité Libre* article "La nouvelle trahison des clercs" (The New Treason of the Intellectuals). The nationalists' answer had come from Hubert Aquin, an achingly bright intellectual who later wrote Quebec's best novel of the 1960s, *Prochain épisode* (Next Episode), a classic in its own right. Aquin mocked Trudeau's theory with biting style. "According to Trudeau, French Canadians are left with the following choice, nothingness or apotheosis," he would write in his equally epoch-making "La fatigue intellectuelle du Canada français" (The Cultural Fatigue of French Canada). "You are either Maurice Richard or nobody."

In that debate, Lévesque's stance was a democratic outlook tinged with nationalism: apotheosis for every Québécois, each according to his or her means. Collective enrichment will lift every man's boat, but for this to happen, the state must shoulder its responsibilities, and nobody is going to do this for us. He also derided Trudeau's view by countering that English Canada would never allow French Canadians to excel. Trudeau responded in kind by laughing off Lévesque's French-speaking electricity.

The Laurendeau salon was thus host to many robust exchanges between the elected doer and the philosopher without a kingdom. One night, while they were talking at Laurendeau's, they heard a loud bang outside, like a bomb exploding. They all went to have a look. A bomb had gone off, indeed. The next day, police confirmed it had been a Front de libération du Québec bomb.

The times, they were a-changing.

CHAPTER THIRTEEN

Fun, Fun, Fun

From 1960 to 1966, Jean Lesage's Quebec was a youngster who had blown his first paycheque on a down payment for a fast car. He also had a brand-new credit card with no spending limit, and he was ready to rock. And rock he did.

There emerged the notion that, since there were no major French-speaking capitalists or industrialists at the time, the state of Quebec would have to fill that role. Hence the flurry of government initiatives that would modernize industry in Quebec and help it achieve the nationalists' long-standing dream of manufacturing and refining the province's natural resources, instead of simply extracting them and then exporting them at advantageous prices for the buyers.

Lévesque was the minister responsible for mines. He would not be able to turn them into Hydro-Québec II, though. Most mines were foreign-owned, 60 percent of them American, and although he managed to increase the royalties they paid, he remained careful not to upset a sector on which thirty thousand jobs depended. Quebec's ore would continue to be refined in Pittsburgh, not Drummondville.

Faced by the impossibility of dramatic action, Lévesque fell back on the creation of government outfits designed to modernize Quebec's economy. It was the heyday of abbreviations: SGF, Société générale de financement, with venture capital to seek investment opportunities; Sidbec, a steel-making company that earned only the dubious distinction of producing the most expensive steel in the world; and Lévesque's own SOQUEM for mining exploration and SOQUIP for gas and oil ventures, both with pretty meagre start-up funds (just $1.5 million a year in the case of SOQUEM). No wonder that, more than forty years later, even the most loyal of Péquistes would be hard-pressed to name even one accomplishment by either company. None of these companies were total failures, but they certainly did not live up to the expectations of their founders, and they cost the Quebec taxpayer an arm and a leg. Thanks to the nationalist sentiment that was so effective at quelling criticism, as in "Yeah, but it's ours, okay? It belongs to us!," successive governments were able to keep these companies afloat without paying too high a political price.

Hydro-Québec, on the other hand, was money well invested. Today it still is a very large and profitable corporation that, unfortunately, covers for a lot of failures born out of the 1960s' state interventionism. Two recent cases in point: the PQ government of Lucien Bouchard and later Bernard Landry invested close to $200 million in the Gaspésia paper mill of Chandler, in the Gaspé. The factory had to close anyway; seven hundred workers lost their jobs, which was a foregone conclusion from the very start, and the installations were dismantled and sold to a Vietnamese company. Yes, Vietnamese. At around the same time, the Quebec government decided to subsidize the already doomed horse-racing industry by creating the Société nationale du cheval de course québécois at a cost of $260 million. No chump change in either case. Quebecers can thank the still-lingering 1960s' mentality for those colossal failures.

IN A FAR MORE EXALTING PURSUIT, the Lesage government took on Ottawa (always a safe target) in the matter of workers' pensions. The very concept of public pensions was then outlandish to most Canadians. It was a benefit known only to the military, public servants, big corporations, and politicians—a minority of the citizenry. However, the idea of a universal pension for workers had been in the air for some time. Ottawa, then under Lester Pearson's Liberals, freshly elected in 1963 after a well-deserved six-year stay in the opposition, had decided to put forth such a plan in addition to the existing Old Age Security, which provides universal benefits for Canadians older than sixty-five years of age. The problem was that Quebec had a similar scheme in mind, and so did Ontario. It became the theme of the Quebec City federal-provincial conference of October 1964.

It was one of those high-drama conferences that news junkies cannot get enough of, a bit like how the Stanley Cup playoffs are for hockey fans. Lesage scored a major goal by producing, out of the blue, a thick document that outlined a detailed workers' pension scheme, much to the fury of some federal officials who had thought that the provinces would have to rally around their own plan. But it was a good document, so much so that Pearson quipped, "Can we join you?" However, Quebec seemed determined to go it alone and not bother with the federal proposal. In the tense atmosphere that settled on the conference, many were predicting the end of the federation as they knew it.

It was, of course, an eminently political gambit that had little to do with the workers' welfare. Pearson's Liberals desperately needed a social measure of the kind that would take them out of minority territory in the House of Commons. As for Lesage, he had been quick to endorse Duplessis's mantle as an autonomist. It was like starting a company under a new name but peddling the same old stuff. Which is all right; all politicians, all parties do that.

The Quebec government had just created the Caisse de dépôt et placement, which brought under the same umbrella a series of small provincial funds. The government's resident economists, chief among them a young Jacques Parizeau, who was to become one of Lévesque's most trusted lieutenants in the Parti Québécois, wanted to enrich the caisse with an automatic feeding scheme. Thanks to the newly created Régie des rentes du Québec, the government would require every Quebecer to surrender 3.5 percent of his or her salary for retirement purposes. Millions would then flow to the caisse every year, and in exchange, workers older than sixty would be guaranteed a pension. The caisse would also become the Quebec government's private bank, free to invest anywhere in the province for the benefit of all residents. Not a bad idea at all, and quite consistent with the nationalists' eternal quest for the perpetual motion that would make Quebec wealthy and independent.

Of course, some Ottawa officials balked: the workers' pension scheme was their brainchild and they wanted to keep it. Then Ontario, following Quebec's example, wanted to go it alone. Things were threatening to unravel. A compromise was reached, thanks in large part to Lesage's deputy minister, Claude Morin, and his Ottawa counter-parts. Quebec and Ottawa agreed to each have their independent pension fund, but with the proviso that they would be universal and "portable." It meant, for instance, that any contributing worker older than sixty who moved from Sudbury, Ontario, to Trois-Rivières, Quebec, would get exactly the same benefits as he would have if he had stayed in his former province. The only difference was that he would get a cheque from Quebec and not Canada; the amounts would be identical. Same thing for a mechanic leaving Sorel, Quebec, for Bathurst, New Brunswick, who would be entitled to his Canada Pension Plan instead of the Régie des rentes du Québec.

Both Pearson and Lesage could claim victory, but the real winner here was the Canadian worker. It was also a rare case of bottom-up standardization of the federation, with a province taking the lead instead of following Ottawa, the natural leader of the pack.

A further word on the standardization of public policy in the Canadian federation: it can be a vertical process, where Ottawa makes decisions based on universal concepts and benefits, with the provinces howling every step of the way before pocketing the money and going along. It can also be very much a horizontal process. For instance, Manitoba women were given the right to vote in 1914, and other provinces followed suit in due time. Driving is another good example. Until the late 1920s, Nova Scotia and British Columbia, in their desire to ape England, "the mother country," forced motorists to drive on the left side of the road, while the opposite side was favoured in other provinces. No wonder there were many car accidents along the Nova Scotia and British Columbia borders. All provinces finally decided, of their own accord and each in its own time, to drive on the right and forget England. Another good example, just for laughs: Prohibition, a First World War child, was enforced unevenly because alcohol comes under provincial jurisdiction. Prince Edward Island was the last to abolish it, in 1946, much to the chagrin of local bootleggers and rum-runners.

In the case of Quebec, though, nationalist ideology makes sure that all such initiatives are presented as *sui generis:* Quebec-made, without any outside influence. It is perhaps one of nationalism's greatest victories: the phony notion that Ottawa and other provinces do not exist, except to cause mischief. Virtually nobody in Quebec knows, for instance, that public health insurance was invented in Saskatchewan or that their province was the last to grant voting rights to Aboriginals at the provincial level, in 1968.

In some regards, the rest of Canada appears to be equally oblivious to what Quebec does well: daycare at seven dollars a day, the generous financial help for parents with young children, the heavy subsidies for senior citizens' homes. All we seem to know about Quebec is the fact that you can buy beer and wine at the corner store.

CHAPTER FOURTEEN

The Dimming Star

Where was Lévesque in the pension debate? He was all for it, of course, cheering the home team from the sidelines—something worth mentioning, because Lévesque sometimes had views of his own that interfered with ministerial solidarity.

In the matter of education reform, for instance, he was seldom heard from. And silence was a rare occurrence for him. Education had always been difficult terrain in Quebec. The Church may have ruled supreme in that domain, but you could not blame her for every woe under the sun. Ever since the French regime, the citizenry had been suspicious of learning. Ratepayers balked at the expense of building schools and paying teachers' salaries. Education was not considered important, unless your family belonged to the local bourgeoisie. School boards were often treated like a joke. In my father's village, the president of the Commission scolaire was a kind man with a fine voice who would sing at mass on Sunday but held his hymn book upside down. Finding good people to run for the school board was sometimes hard, and if you were appointed to the board and turned down the job, you were liable to be fined.

Since 1960, education had been high on the government's list of priorities. Lesage had entrusted the much-needed reform to the man who was probably the most distinguished of all Quiet Revolutionaries, Deputy Premier Paul Gérin-Lajoie, a former Rhodes Scholar who held a doctorate in law.

Gérin-Lajoie got to work in earnest and did his best not to upset the apple cart. True to Canadian tradition, he created a commission to lay the groundwork for the reform, and he tried to assuage all institutions involved before moving ahead. Before Bill 60, the education reform bill, was introduced in the Legislative Assembly in 1964, he toured Quebec for two and a half months to gain support, in which he was successful. His feat was certainly comparable to René Lévesque's campaign for the nationalization of electricity. But when he did move ahead, no matter how careful he was, people thought the government was trying to do too much, too fast, too soon, and with too little. Bringing a rather quaint society into the twentieth century was a monumental endeavour in itself, and the new education ministry complicated things by sometimes proceeding in a typically French, Cartesian fashion, with centralized decision-making that paid little heed to the citizenry. A classic case of a government devoted to the common good but not enough to common sense.

All of a sudden, all Quebecers under the age of twenty-one were swooped up in the education machine. Education was now compulsory and free. Hundreds of schools had to be built, thousands of teachers hired. New institutions galore were created, chief among them the many Collège d'enseignement général et professionnel, the CEGEPs, modelled on American community colleges. Universities were suddenly besieged by hordes of students with bursaries. It was chaos, the free-for-all of the century. Every Quebecer who lived through it has fond and not-so-fond memories of those tumultuous times.

Hiring, for instance. Anybody and everybody could be hired to teach. "So, young man, you are a philosophy graduate. Good for you. Now, we need a teacher of English and physical education. Tell me, can you swim? Yes? So you'll do all right. And I'm sure you know some Beatles songs. You know, 'I Wanna Hold Your Hand,' stuff like that? Excellent. You got a class awaiting you right now, so leave your bag here. Oh, yes, for your training in didactics, well, we'll see about that another time. Good luck!" Yellow school buses started appearing all over the place, convents and seminaries were converted overnight into "*polyvalentes*" and CEGEPs. A lot of people were happy: they could finally imagine a future for their kids away from the farm or the factory. A lot of people were unhappy, too: forced schooling was no fun if your family had been illiterate for eight generations without ever feeling ashamed, especially if there was a well-paid job waiting for you in the resources sector. There were some lamentable failures, and some resounding successes too, depending on the means and the goodwill of those involved.

Lévesque had had his doubts from the start. In his mind, you could nationalize electricity but not teaching and learning. And he rightfully wondered where the province would find the thousands of teachers needed for the reform. In the end, however, he kept quiet about his reservations and supported the government. It seems that he saved his doubts for his memoirs, where he excoriated the Quebec education system.

There were other instances where he was not always onside. When confronted one day by liquor control board employees on strike, he told them to "hang in there." The premier was not amused. For years, Lesage had tolerated Lévesque as the *enfant terrible* of the government. He would forgive his star minister for his frequent sleeping in and his subsequent late arrival at Cabinet meetings, for he knew Lévesque worked hard and contributed much to the government's good standings in the polls. Lesage's patience was wearing thin, though. Other ministers were annoyed at Lévesque's propensity to hog all the attention. Not everyone had forgiven him for claiming at a gathering of nationalists in 1964: "The only status that would suit Quebec is the status of an associated state within the Canadian federation, something we will have to negotiate with the rest of Canada, without guns or dynamite. And if they turn us down, then yes, Quebec will have to separate." Lesage and his entourage were furious.

But Lévesque was oblivious to criticism. He was having fun. His political persona was already set. He was the minister who always said yes to an interview request, never turned down an opportunity to address an audience, had an opinion to share on just about everything. The minister always on the run, with stacks of files under his arm, who had all the time in the world for his advisers and senior civil servants but would often miss appointments. He was busy— and enjoying it.

He was not yet a separatist. To him, separatism was a concept for the hotheaded dreamers of Bourgault's Rassemblement pour l'indépendance nationale, who had read too much for their own good, or for the melancholy right-wing history professors struggling to rejuvenate Canon Groulx's teachings. Lévesque had evolved into a positive nationalist, working for the good of all Quebecers, not just French-speaking ones.

He had also discovered the North, a region almost non-existent in Quebecers' imagination, save for then-little-read Yves Thériault novels. His duties as minister of natural resources had taken him there. He was annoyed by the fact that the French presence was invisible in northern Quebec and the fact that Aboriginal life was dominated by the federal government and a few companies, like the Hudson's Bay Company (HBC). He met with the Cree and the Inuit and listened to their grievances. The Aboriginals' living conditions reminded him of his native Gaspé, with the HBC enjoying a monopoly on purchasing pelts and providing basic goods. Also, he could not help but notice the Aboriginals' political disenfranchisement. He resented the fact that Ottawa occupied too much space in the North, but then Quebec had so far shown little interest in Ungava, James Bay, and the Arctic. Lévesque was determined to change the course of things, which would mean inevitable battles with Ottawa, but he did not mind that.

He was not up there long enough to make any meaningful changes, but he did what he could. He petitioned Cabinet to allow Aboriginals to vote at the provincial level, and he proposed opening schools where the language of instruction would be Cree or Inuktitut. In short, what Lévesque wanted for the Québécois, he wanted for Aboriginal minorities in the province, too. This was a clear case where the democrat in him spoke louder than the nationalist: Quebec's particularism should be respectful of others' particularisms. Interestingly, though, René Lévesque's legend rarely mentions his positive relations with Aboriginals.

SO TIMES WERE GOOD. But not for long.

On October 14, 1965, Lesage cracked the whip: Lévesque lost his Natural Resources portfolio and was appointed minister of family and welfare. He was not alone in experiencing what was widely seen as a fall from grace. Eric Kierans, a former academic and successful businessman turned politician (a *rara avis*) and Lévesque's most trusted ally in Cabinet, was ejected from Revenue and landed in Health. Many in the Liberal Party were elated. It was thought that, by assigning them social portfolios, Lesage had finally put his foot down and given his two high-profile ministers a much-deserved lesson in humility.

Lévesque seemed to take it in stride. It simply looked like a new challenge. Quite the challenge, as it turned out. He had, in effect, become minister of the downtrodden. He was soon to discover the plight of handicapped people in the countryside hidden by their families, Quebec's crowded orphanages, the fact that 40 percent of families lived in dire poverty in Montreal alone. He brought to the task the same energy he had deployed at Natural Resources, only his new responsibilities attracted less attention and, moreover, less financial support from government. This was the era when the Church was slowly exiting the social field. When Lévesque claimed that social needs were so great that "Quebec must substitute solidarity for charity," his comment did not cause the stir it would have just three years earlier. Here, too, he thought that part of the solution resided in Ottawa, which is why he proposed the repatriation of family allowances from Ottawa. But picking a political fight was no remedy for the host of social problems he had to contend with.

So the task was not much fun, not like nationalizing electricity. And knowing that he himself had entrusted the care of his daughter born out of wedlock to her mother's more capable hands, Lévesque must have felt like Jean-Jacques Rousseau abandoning his children to orphanages at the very time he was composing *Émile*, his treatise on the education of children. This was definitely not the kind of part he felt was for him.

Lévesque stayed only a few months in Family and Welfare. An election had been called for June 5, 1966.

CHAPTER FIFTEEN

The Wilderness

Many otherwise intelligent men mistakenly believe that because their wives are in love with them they surely cannot be as clever as they themselves are. Such men sometimes come home from a golf game, slightly inebriated and chewing on a cigar, only to find the car gone and the locks changed. On the porch are two neatly packed bags with a note that says: Get a lawyer. It happens so often. Especially to overconfident politicians. It happened to Jean Lesage. He had been premier for six years and the spouse in this case was the electorate—who had had enough.

He was baffled. After all, had he not brought much-needed change to the province? Well, yes, and maybe that was the problem: there had been too much change, and the voters were looking for a respite. Lesage's opponent, UN's reassuringly bland Daniel Johnson, had led a shrewd campaign, concentrating on the rural regions and avoiding any debate with the more skilled Lesage. The Liberal premier had not helped his cause by running a de Gaulle–like campaign, with all the attention being focused on him. He had taken away most of the thunder from his "*équipe du tonnerre*" in order to shine like the Sun King.

But there was more. Quebecers had a still-new Liberal government in Ottawa, and they seemed to feel that one Liberal government was enough. As well, voters had matured and appeared to be ready to taste the joys of what in French is called *alternance;* that is, voting in a new party every eight years or so. They have been pretty consistent about it for almost forty years now: two terms seems to be the limit. Other provinces have followed suit—Ontario, for example, once the Tory dynasty had come to an end after Bill Davis's departure in 1985. The only exception remains Alberta, where voters alternate every half-century or so.

Lévesque had been re-elected in Laurier. He did not know it, but he had started ten years in purgatory.

OPPOSITION IS FOR COMMITTED PARLIAMENTARIANS. It is serious work. There is no better place to hone your skills as a politician. If you are new to the legislature and thus spared the burden of governance, it is a good time to learn about procedure, committee work, and speech making. If you have been in power before, and if the former opposition now in office has the gall to appropriate your old policies and simply rebrand them as their own—as most parties do in Canada—now is the time to show your mettle.

Of course it is never easy to criticize what you yourself were doing only yesterday and to deride with gusto precisely what you yourself had planned to do. It is often an unpleasant and antagonistic game in which you are required to laugh off or pillory fine ideas that would have been yours if an ungrateful electorate had not sent you packing. Now is also the time to be patient, a virtue that does not come easily to formerly powerful government members who become the powerless governed overnight. You can only find solace in the thought that if you are returned to office some day, you will be more adept at governing. Opposition is the best of schools if you are shrewd, ambitious, and, I repeat, patient.

But Lévesque was the most impatient man in Quebec. The new UN government had decided to let Liberal reforms take their course, so he could hardly take the new administration to task. Daniel Johnson, who had been in both government and opposition, would only smile when indignant Liberals attacked him for what they had planned to do themselves. It was his turn to have fun. And of course, wise as he was, Johnson not only poached the Liberals' ideas and voters, he also made sure that the UN faithful were silenced into submission with juicy appointments and symbolic gestures. In that respect, Johnson was a real Canadian politician in the true sense of the word.

All of this made Lévesque miserable. He had no taste for procedural games and was loath to criticize his former self. He was a democrat all right, a politician, of course, but an indifferent parliamentarian. He had better things to do, and, naturally, one of the rare luxuries of being in opposition is that you have a lot of time on your hands. Some use it to reflect or get reacquainted with their families, others to plot changes within the party leadership or to conspire. Lévesque certainly did not "spend more time with his family" or conspire, but he used his time well.

Foremost on his mind was Quebec's place in the federation. It was a time when independence was in the air all over the place. Africa and Asia were shaking old colonial chains. Only four years earlier, in 1962, Algeria had finally achieved independence from France after a long and bloody struggle. The United Nations was greeting new members almost every day. Daniel Johnson's UN had even gotten into the game by publishing its manifesto *Equality or Independence* in 1965. Nothing too radical, just the old autonomist thesis somewhat rejuvenated, along with a profession of faith in blackmail. But still, the I-word had been used. What had seemed like pure folly only two years earlier was starting to make sense for a lot of people, and not just starry-eyed idealists and aging crackpots.

Now a seasoned politician, Lévesque could clearly see that the concept of independence was gaining ground on the right, with Johnson's people, and was already well implanted on the left, with Bourgault's RIN. So if the Quebec Liberal Party wanted to remain relevant, it had to move in that direction. He and others in the party had already mused publicly about Quebec as an associated state. More and more, he felt that it was the way out of a weak and sterile opposition; the future pointed in that direction.

He had other equally radical ideas. For instance, why not do away with slush funds and thus free all political parties from the influence of money? Why not have equal airtime for all parties in any election? Why not have public tenders everywhere in government? Why not open up the appointment process? This way, the QLP could reinvent itself as a clean, modern party, starkly different from the old UN, and at the same time teach the young RIN a lesson in political morality. Those were the ideas of a politician hoping to keep his natural audience and enlarge it by mining his opponents' backyards.

Lévesque managed to build a group around him that dealt with these issues in earnest. One member was young

Robert Bourassa, a trained economist and the new member for Mercier in the Legislative Assembly. This was the group that came up with the idea of sovereignty-association. Unlike so many opposition members unhappy with Lesage's leadership, who were blaming the leader for their loss to the UN, Lévesque did not want to change leaders. He wanted his leader and his party to change. A tall order, but he thought he could pull it off: after all, he had convinced Lesage and his Cabinet to nationalize hydro. But hydro was policy; sovereignty was high-stakes politics.

Then came de Gaulle. During his visit to Expo 67 in Montreal, he shouted his famous, or infamous, "Vive le Québec libre!" Lévesque was in the crowd that day, but he was not as impressed as the many young RIN militants who were in awe of de Gaulle. His reaction was subdued; in a way, he was grateful for the prestigious *coup de pouce,* but felt it somehow smacked of benevolent imperialism. He believed Quebecers could manage on their own, thank you very much, and that they did not need the endorsement of a foreign republic that still owned colonies. In his own way, Lévesque was reacting like a French Canadian already free and independent for more than three centuries, while many of his future comrades-in-arms were fawning all over de Gaulle like affection-starved colonists. Liberal MLA

François Aquin even endorsed de Gaulle's words and quit the QLP to sit as an independent.

In the fall, René Lévesque was ready to make his move. He had a booklet ready, *Option Québec,* in which he expounded his new political views. His hour of reckoning in the QLP was nearing. The party's convention was to take place on October 13, 1967, in Quebec City. He knew that many card-carrying Liberals, chief among them party president Eric Kierans, were to tell Lévesque that if he persisted in his new ways, he would no longer be welcome in the party.

Things were not going well for him. Some members of his group had already bolted. They included Robert Bourassa, who told Lévesque, after much soul-searching, that you could not have political independence and monetary union at the same time. Which made sense—except to Lévesque, who could see nothing wrong with his bold new plan.

He could hardly be blamed for that. The late 1960s and the early 1970s were not so much trying times as times for trying. After all, there was so much upheaval in the world, why not try this or that? It was 1967, the year of Expo, when Canadians tried just about everything: pre-marital sex, pot, French cheese, wine, bell-bottom pants, and an Italian dish called pizza. Canada was about to elect as their prime minister Lévesque's favourite foe, Pierre Trudeau, whose persona embodied the advent of a new order. Leonard Cohen, Joni Mitchell, Robertson Davies, and Margaret Atwood were about to come into their own. Québécois singers and writers were making their mark everywhere in the world. British, French, and American hegemony in Canadian culture was being challenged. It did not stop there: a Quebec-made sports car, the Manic, saw the light of day in 1969. New Brunswick's Bricklin would follow in 1974. Both cars now sit in museums, but at least someone had been bold enough to try to realize their dream.

So René Lévesque's sovereignty-association was very much in keeping with the times. He was simply trying something out. And in the Canadian political lexicon, it was only one more oxymoron (the most durable one being the Progressive Conservative Party of Canada).

At the October 13, 1967, Liberal policy convention, Lévesque moved that the party hold a secret ballot on his proposals. His motion was turned down. He then saw that his faction was a minority, powerless to move the party forward. He stormed out of the convention hall followed by a handful of supporters, some of them in tears. Lévesque had gambled and lost. It was his first major political defeat. He was heartbroken.

CHAPTER SIXTEEN

MSA

Heartbroken, but not for long: that very evening in Quebec City, surrounded by the few friends who had left the QLP with him, Lévesque started mapping out the future.

What happened next is a story with rich biblical overtones. Lévesque's drama was all over the news. Suddenly, the idea of Quebec independence had gained respectability. After all, he was a sitting member of the Legislative Assembly, he had been in Cabinet, he had accomplished things, and he had retained the trust of many. Not that everybody was going to join him right away, but at least he had credibility. And he could benefit from the fact that, all of a sudden, his former home, the QLP, looked tired and averse to change. The UN already was despairingly old hat. As for the overtly separatist RIN, although they had fared respectably in the 1966 elections, with almost 6 percent of the popular vote, nobody in their right mind would have bet a dime on their future. It was the same for the other separatist parties, all of them stuck on the fringe. And the FLQ, still active, was feared. Not Lévesque. So now was the time to move on and gain some momentum. He and his small group of disaffected Liberals got to work.

On November 18 and 19, 1967, barely a month after the ill-fated QLP convention, a group of diehard Lévesque followers gathered at the Dominican monastery in Outremont, except that they now numbered four hundred. Donations had already started to pour in: one-dollar bills, five-dollar bills, a ten, even the odd twenty here and there, money that usually came with a handwritten letter of encouragement that took the form of a profession of faith in Quebec and in Lévesque. Not truckloads of money, but clean money, no strings attached.

Bent on ideological as well as financial purity, Lévesque's disciples refused to call themselves a party. Their tent would be a large one. Action-oriented people and visionaries alike would join hands in the interest of one common goal: to redefine Quebec's place in Canada. It would be an innovative pursuit: sovereignty but also association with Canada. And if that were not possible, perhaps full independence. So it would be a movement, not a party. Its name, chosen by Lévesque, was to be the Mouvement Souveraineté-Association, MSA for short.

The choice of the gathering place was highly symbolic, although no one noticed at the time. Quebec was undergoing a massive mutation, moving silently from a highly moral, Church-ridden society to a secular, hedonistic one. Vatican II, in the early 1960s, had loosened restrictions a little. Catholics were now allowed to eat meat on Fridays and no longer had to fast three hours before taking Holy Communion. But as soon as the door was ajar, the whole flock rushed out and scattered. In Quebec, disaffection with the Church took the form of a quiet recantation—nothing spectacular, no fanfare, no loud speeches. Quite the Canadian way, when you think of it. Attendance at mass dwindled with each passing month; confessionals were no longer besieged; priests, brothers, and sisters were leaving their orders in droves. You might run into your former parish priest, a man whose stern looks, black cassock, and white Roman collar had put the fear of God into you when you were a child. But he was now dressed in civvies, and he would introduce you to his companion, a woman you would recognize as the now-former nun who had taught you in grade school. He had chastised you at confession for taking a suspiciously long shower, and she had rapped your fingers for saying a dirty word. They would blush and give you an awkward smile, almost begging forgiveness but not quite, and go on their merry way. It happened all the time. People no longer asked the bishop for permission to read forbidden books; the pill was available; mind and body had been set free.

Nature abhors a vacuum? So does belief. The MSA did not lack zealots to take the faith to the heathen. After a lot of meetings in now-idle church basements, the missionaries of the new movement had made 7,800 converts. Some 1,700 delegates met for their first convention, a sort of Eucharistic affair, on April 19, 1968, at the Maurice Richard Arena. Again a symbolic choice: political fervour had supplanted religious élan and had found a home in an arena (a term that, like *Dominican,* originated in ancient Rome) dedicated to the half-god of Quebec's other religion, hockey.

But trouble came early in paradise. While working on the bylaws of the MSA, François Aquin, the MLA who had approved of General de Gaulle's call for the liberation of Quebec, found himself at odds with Lévesque's ideal of sovereignty-association, and he was not alone in his dissent. It was a strict matter of logic, they said: it is independence you must strive for, and once that is achieved, you determine the kind of links you want to have with the outside world. It made sense; after all, you cannot leave and stay at the same time. It was the first time anyone had dared to challenge Lévesque's audacious new concepts.

Needless to say, he was unhappy, for he knew in his soul that Quebecers were not ready for this journey into the unknown called independence. Lévesque felt he could accurately gauge the people's pulse, that he had his ear to the ground. Too many people would instinctively turn away from the new political gospel of the hour; it was too radical. Lévesque also felt that idealists like Aquin had not thought enough about Talleyrand's clever definition of democracy, which can be paraphrased as follows: There is someone in France who is more clever than Voltaire, more clever than Bonaparte, more clever than any of our ministers, past, present, or future, and that someone is everybody. Lévesque just knew that not everybody was onside yet. You had to proceed with caution, reassure the public, tell them they would lose nothing, only gain. So it would be political independence along with economic security, period.

But how do you quell the dissent of the few while maintaining the faith of the many? Only a politician with street smarts could pull it off. That was a job for Lévesque. It was also the first opportunity he had to put his stamp on his new political party.

Aquin's supporters made a mistake, and Lévesque pounced on it. They had moved that, in an independent Quebec, "public funding would be limited strictly to

French-language schools." No more subsidies for English schools, Jewish schools, private schools, nothing. Lévesque immediately said no. "The Quebec I want," he said, "will be pluralist, tolerant, and respectful of minorities" (a bit like today's Canada). "But if the convention wishes to pass that resolution," he went on, "I shall have to think about my future involvement in a movement that bears my name. I can always go back home and stay there," he concluded. The disciples were shocked, and many reasoned they could not afford to lose their prophet. So they voted down the proposal, and that marked their support for the idea of sovereignty-association. It was the first time that Lévesque had used his immense prestige to stare down a vocal minority. He had opened the door and said, "Dare me." The faithful had gathered around him in short order, and the dissidents were left with one choice: take a bow or take a hike.

So not everyone was elated, but that happens every time you have a major policy disagreement in a party. And if dissenters are not strong enough to challenge the establishment, they either walk away noisily or fade away quietly. Either way, they are seldom heard from afterwards. By the summer of 1968, Aquin was gone, a has-been forever. Lévesque was the Boss. The idealistic altar boys had been bulldozed by the wily politician basking in the affection of his supporters. Many more tough episodes of this sort lay ahead, but there would be only one boss, and that was René Lévesque.

Had he blackmailed the MSA into recanting ideological purity out of his love for minorities, or was he motivated by unadulterated political crassness? No matter; it was, to be sure, one of those times when nationalism in Lévesque's thinking would take a back seat to democracy. He had also dealt fanaticism a major blow by convincing his new political family that tolerance was, in fact, the real vote-rich territory.

Lévesque's political brand was now established. He would stand squarely in the middle of the nationalist political spectrum: away from the France-inspired right-wing ideology that had been conservative nationalism's trademark, and away from Third World liberation theology, another import that had become the left's new credo. Like Louis-Joseph Papineau a century earlier, who had dreamed of achieving home rule without shedding blood, Lévesque vowed that his quest for Quebec's sovereignty would be a peaceful struggle. The quest for sovereignty-association would be waged from the centre, the only political avenue that has any future in Canada.

CHAPTER SEVENTEEN

PQ

Lévesque's MSA was soon casting its net ever wider, bringing in voters with separatist leanings. The other small fringe parties were bleeding, their members flocking over to Lévesque's movement. The first who came calling with offers of a merger was the Ralliement national (RN) headed by Gilles Grégoire, a former Social Credit MP. His members were salt-of-the-earth kind of people but very conservative in their outlook: prosperous habitants and small businessmen from the Quebec *terroir* who had never warmed to what they called the "old parties," Liberals and Conservatives, and adhered to a more Quebec-centric political order.

As soon as word of talks between the MSA and the RN got around, Pierre Bourgault's RIN went soul-searching. Many in his party disliked Lévesque, finding him too bourgeois. They wanted a French socialist republic on the St. Lawrence, not an associated state within Canada. But the leader himself was not so sure. Bourgault had enough political sense to see that his membership was dwindling, so he hoped to conclude a formal merger with the MSA that would give more muscle to the left-leaning forces within the separatist movement. And it would give him the clout he felt was commensurate with his oratorical genius and unlimited skills. But he did not want to ask. He decided to wait for Lévesque's overtures.

Lévesque was under pressure within the MSA to join forces with the RIN, or to at least talk to Bourgault, but he would not budge: he felt that the RIN was too radical for most Quebecers and that it was also too closely associated with the bomb-planting Front de libération du Québec (FLQ, or Quebec Liberation Front). Lévesque did not want to be in any way associated with that. And, wily as ever, he knew that the RIN members would come to him anyway, so why give Bourgault a status within the movement he was sure to use to his advantage? Let him wait.

Then came the June 24, 1968, Saint-Jean-Baptiste Day parade in Montreal. The federal election was set to take place the following day, June 25. The parade was an important event, with Radio-Canada's cameras and microphones everywhere. Which was why Bourgault and some of his colleagues in the RIN had planned to turn the parade into a riot. Their aim was to show that mainstream Quebec would from now on be rejecting Canada and its new leader.

What occurred was classic political theatre, featuring the victory of genuine spontaneity over ill-advised planning. When Pierre Trudeau, the prime minister-designate, took his seat in the stands as the guest of honour, he was readily greeted by jeers and a few flying bottles of beer. But when all hell seemed to break loose, he refused to leave his seat and told his bodyguards to go help the other fleeing guests instead. He stared down the separatist rioters. In that instant, he embodied the youthful boldness the country might need in the troubled times ahead.

Bourgault had also planned that, as soon as trouble was underway, his followers would let the rumour fly that he had been arrested, so as to infuriate the crowd and heighten the protest. It did not exactly turn out that way. The Montreal Police had been keeping an eye on Bourgault from the start, and he was soon surrounded by police officers in civvies, whom he mistook for RIN supporters. Surrounded by suspiciously zealous admirers who were chanting his name, Bourgault, still waving to the crowd, was walked straight into the awaiting paddy wagon. In his cell at the police station, he waited in vain for the delirious crowd to free him.

As for Trudeau, he was handily elected the next day. Sure, there were other factors at work in his election, but anyone could see that Trudeau had the physical courage to confront the separatists. A reassuring sight for many. In the following days, Lévesque was able to convince the party faithful and the general public that he had good reasons to stay away from the megalomaniacal Bourgault and his rowdy supporters. Bourgault was then isolated.

In the end, both Trudeau and Lévesque used the Saint-Jean-Baptiste Day riot to achieve their goals: the former to solidify his image as a separatist fighter who would not blink; the latter to portray himself as the reasonable sovereignist alternative. Poor Bourgault, the only one in the trio who was not a true politician, ended up with the part of the tough-luck Pierrot in the *commedia dell'arte* pantomimes, left behind on the sidewalk in the middle of the night, gazing at the two shooting stars, René and the other Pierre.

ON OCTOBER 11, 1968, the RN and the MSA congregated at the Coliseum (another word evocative of Rome's erstwhile power) in Quebec City to form the Parti Québécois (PQ). Lévesque did not much like the name, for it sounded a little too nationalist to his taste, but he went along in the end. He was elected president of the PQ.

Bourgault was not around, of course, and he had given up waiting for a formal invitation. But he did not go quietly.

A few days before the merger, at his party's own gathering, he moved that the RIN disband in order to join forces with the new sovereignist party. He himself would join the PQ, and he invited his followers to do the same en masse. That way, the left wing of the nationalist movement could hope to at least influence Lévesque's party. Bourgault would be only a foot soldier in the new army, but he would remain a thorn in the side of the man who had dared treat him with contempt.

In Quebec's still-Catholic culture, Bourgault's gesture of abnegation was well received. This way, Bourgault was sure to remain a central figure in their affection, which was perhaps the only thing he wanted after all. As for Lévesque, Bourgault's self-sacrifice did not move him one bit: he was the founding father of the PQ and the beloved son at the same time. He did not even bother to thank Bourgault. He was, once again, the sole master in the house of his making.

CHAPTER EIGHTEEN

Turbulent Years

September 1969. Saint-Léonard was a quiet, little-known suburb of Montreal. Italian immigrants had settled there in droves, and, not surprisingly, they wanted their children to be educated in the majority language of their new country. They and other immigrants to Quebec were not fools: they could see that Quebec's French-speakers did not enjoy the same standard of living as their English-speaking counterparts. Sure, they were willing to speak the language of the majority at work, but they did not even contemplate allowing their children to be educated in French.

Members of the Saint-Léonard school board, some of them card-carrying nationalists, noticed with increasing alarm that immigrants were shunning French schools in favour of English ones, so they decided to block access to English schools and force them into French ones. This would reverse a trend that many Quebecers feared: a growing linguistic minority and a shrinking French majority.

The result was a sometimes violent standoff between two schools of thought. The first was the nationalist view, which held that individuals and minorities must bow to the will of the majority. The situation was compounded by two factors. One was that you were dealing with immigrants; it was not their country, so they would do as they were told, period. The other factor was the regular publication of statistics in the French-language press that dwelt on the decreasing French population of Canada. If we do nothing, demographers moaned, we will first become a minority in the only territory we can call our own, Quebec, and then we will disappear slowly as a nation. These predictions touched a raw nerve in nationalist circles, a historical insecurity that had its roots in the seventeenth-century Iroquois wars, the perennial complaints of the governors of New France about the woeful lack of colonists, the threatening presence of the powerful and populated New England colonies in the eighteenth century, and the departure in the nineteenth century of some eight thousand French Canadians, who were forced into working for a pittance and a roof over their heads in U.S. mill towns. In the 1920s, Lionel Groulx and his supporters were already predicting the imminent demise of French Canada.

Quebec had survived it all and was now six million strong, but brushes with extinction were very much on the mind of any educated Québécois. Now the threat was new, and it seemed to come from within. Many felt that something had to be done about immigration. And it was not just a matter of countering assimilation; it was also a novel case of a majority that had always thought of itself as a minority suddenly realizing its strength and wanting for the first time in its history to assert itself. The message was clear: this is our place, always has been, and from now on, we will manage our own affairs in accordance with our aspirations.

At the same time, an old Canadian school of thought emerged in a new way: the idea that minorities might have rights, that individuals did not have to bow to the will of the majority. Italian immigrants were saying to school authorities in Saint-Léonard, "We are in Canada here, and we are entitled to an education in the language of our choice." At the same time, countless French-speaking parents in Ontario, Manitoba, and New Brunswick were saying to their school boards: "Listen, we have rights too, we've been here for centuries, and for years we have been deprived of education in our own language, so now we want it. And we want it now!" Minorities were asserting themselves against unjust majorities.

Politicians of all stripes were perplexed, of course. One who surveyed the field with a keen eye was Pierre Trudeau. Upon entering politics, he had said that his aim was to protect the individual against the tyranny of the group, the minority against the majority. Another was Lévesque, who had never really indulged in the demagoguery of apprehension about Quebec's disappearance. He wanted a Quebec that would be very much like, well, Trudeau's Canada, that is, dynamic *and* respectful of minorities. But then, he could also understand the anguish felt by many francophones in the face of self-anglicizing immigration. There was one other thing, and it was a little embarrassing: he, too, had been schooled in English in his early years, and that had been not only his meal ticket but also his ticket out of a narrow and stifling Quebec. So he struggled in search of a solution.

Meanwhile things were turning ugly in Saint-Léonard. There were successive clashes pitting militant nationalists and angry Italian parents. Many people were injured, and Quebecers saw on TV images of violence they never thought they'd see in their own backyard. At one point, five hundred policemen with helmets and sticks were needed to quell a riot. It was all very unsettling.

The UN government, now headed by Jean-Jacques Bertrand, who had taken the helm after Daniel Johnson's death in 1968, decided to settle the matter, Duplessis-style. Since children belonged to parents, it would be up to the family, not the government, to decide which school the kids should attend. Immigrants were elated, and so were many French-speaking parents who wanted their offspring to be educated in English "so that they would have a leg up in life." A bit like René Lévesque himself.

Bill 63, the act that let parents choose the language of education for their children, was passed overwhelmingly by the newly christened National Assembly, with the support of the UN and the Liberals. Lévesque and a few others voted the other way. It was a defeat for him, but a victory of sorts, too. Because now, thanks to the reawakening of the old demons of nativist insecurity, many Québécois who were formerly indifferent to the fate of the nation were squarely in his camp. That would help Lévesque's cause immensely, even though he very seldom used this new arrow in his quiver, for he knew in his heart of hearts that insecurity is a close cousin of intolerance.

APRIL 29, 1970. Election time again. A three-way race this time: an uneasy Jean-Jacques Bertrand heading the UN; the thirty-six-year-old economist Robert Bourassa, who had replaced Jean Lesage, as captain of the Liberals; and Lévesque with his fresh and battle-eager PQ. Bourassa and his economic cure-all gospel for Quebec's political and social woes won the contest hands down. Still favoured by the electoral map in the rural ridings, the UN would form the Official Opposition. As for the PQ, it had done quite well, with 23 percent of the popular vote, although this translated into only seven seats in the National Assembly. Among the newly elected were twenty-three-year-old former student leader Claude Charron, TV psychiatrist Camille Laurin, and flamboyant union lawyer Robert Burns.

Lévesque had lost his riding of Laurier. When the faithful gathered that night, there was electricity in the air, as well as palpable disappointment. He had to find the right words to calm the crowd. As usual, he was up to the task: "Don't you think this defeat looks a lot like a moral victory?" he intoned. And he proceeded to remind his audience that their young party had done a lot in a few years with few resources; the future could only be better. Everybody calmed down right away, and after the gathering, they all went home quietly. No windows broken, no brawls with *les Anglais,* nothing. It was a convincing manifestation of Lévesque's moral clout—that is, using the power of the word for the benefit of democracy—and it bore the mark of the kind of moral dignity that paves the way to undisputed victories.

That night, there was a young reporter in the audience, Don Macpherson of *The Gazette*. Fifteen years later, when Lévesque stepped down as premier, Macpherson wrote,

"The first time I covered Lévesque, he averted a riot." That's the kind of eulogy fit for a great artist of democracy.

THE MOST IMMEDIATE QUESTION on Lévesque's mind was, Where will my next meal come from? He was entitled to a parliamentary pension, but he quickly surrendered it to his wife, whom he had, by this time, finally left for good. Since Louise Lévesque had the care of the children, René had also relinquished his house in Outremont to her.

As usual, he was indifferent. The fact that he was in love helped. She was Corinne Côté, a strapping beauty from Lac-Saint-Jean, much younger and taller than he, but that, he could live with. She would become his companion for life, although he never mended his Don Juan ways. Ever lucky, he was rescued from famine by the press baron Pierre Péladeau, who hired him as a columnist for the *Journal de Montréal* at two hundred dollars a week. So things were looking up. Then came summer, and soothing days with Corinne on a New England beach.

TRAGEDY STRUCK IN THE FALL. It began on October 5, with the abduction by the FLQ of Great Britain's trade commissioner in Montreal, James Richard Cross. Lévesque was taken aback at first. "These kids got guts," was his initial comment, although he evidently did not approve. Cross's kidnapping sent tremors throughout Canada. Nobody here was used to this; things like that happened elsewhere: on television, for instance. The situation took a turn for the worse when Quebec's labour minister, Pierre Laporte, was abducted too, from his home on October 10, with his children watching. Canadians were stunned again, but Quebecers even more so. This was someone they knew, and his name was a common one; it was as if every family had been touched personally. And the FLQ members were local boys. How could they? Quebec had woken up in the middle of a foreign movie, but one with familiar actors and surroundings. The kidnapping was particularly traumatic for René Lévesque, who had known Laporte for almost twenty years, first as a journalist and later as a fellow MNA and minister in Lesage's government.

Ever the politician, Lévesque sought to insulate his PQ from the FLQ. There was no link between his quest for sovereignty and the creation of an independent Workers' Republic of Quebec by violent means. But in the turmoil that ensued, such distinctions were easily blurred in the public's mind. He soon joined what was called the Committee of Sixteen, a group of eminent citizens who wanted the government of Quebec to negotiate with the hostage-takers. In Ottawa, Pierre Trudeau was adamant in his refusal: you do not talk to common criminals, you arrest them, try them, and jail them, end of story.

Events would soon overtake Lévesque. On October 15, the National Assembly petitioned the federal government to enact the War Measures Act; Ottawa obliged on October 16. The next day, October 17, Pierre Laporte's body was found in the trunk of an abandoned car. The whole province, indeed the whole country, reeled. Lévesque was crushed. After struggling to compose a press release in which he condemned Laporte's assassins in no uncertain terms, he withdrew and broke down in tears. At that very moment, in Ottawa, alone with his fiancée, Margaret Sinclair, Pierre Trudeau was crying too.

Lévesque rebounded quickly. In his columns in the *Journal de Montréal* in the days that followed, he regularly excoriated Trudeau for what he termed an excessive reaction to the events. He then went into overdrive. He decried the army's presence so much, derided Bourassa's perceived weakness so fiercely, blamed Trudeau so forcefully that, in the end, he forgot who the real criminals were. Even after Cross was freed and Laporte's murderers were jailed, he persisted in saying that Trudeau had used the October Crisis to consolidate his position in Quebec, weaken the Bourassa government, and, above all, destroy the sovereignist movement. In his defence, one can only say that he knew what he was talking about: after all, he had used the 1968 Saint-Jean-Baptiste Day riot to sabotage his rival Pierre Bourgault and the RIN.

Overall, Lévesque's take on the October Crisis was a political gambit of the vilest sort. He was not seeking the truth; he was only trying to regain the political terrain he had lost. The polls were not good: 81 percent of Quebecers were in favour of the War Measures Act. And in the few months that followed, 45 percent of the PQ membership vanished. His party was hurting, but that was a poor excuse for resorting to such crass partisanship over a dead friend's body.

In shifting not so subtly the responsibility for the October Crisis, Lévesque unwittingly gave birth to a cottage industry of sorts in Quebec: a whole slew of revisionist theories around the events, all of them based on Lévesque's rant that the blame should be put on Trudeau. The conspiracy theorists went so far as to say that everything had in fact been orchestrated from the start by Ottawa's secret police (that would be the RCMP, which is giving our national police a lot of credit ...), abetted by the CIA. Come to think of it, Laporte's murderer was Trudeau, no one else.

I cannot say that the general public has bought these foolish ideas wholesale, but one thing is certain: it is politically correct nowadays in the nationalist milieu to say that Laporte "died," which is a curious way to describe Paul Rose's strangling of the minister with the chain of his scapular medal. But using the word *died* instead of the word *murdered* keeps Laporte's abductors absolved. As in "our boys couldn't do that, only bad Ottawa and the CIA." I would not be at all surprised if people started saying one day that, in fact, Laporte was "deceased."

Sad to say, but what the scribbler politician in Lévesque launched here was a process in which intellectual dishonesty joined forces with political expediency, the effect of which was to absolve the guilty and have criminals trade places with victims. It was a pretty callous perversion of historical truth, and a technique Lévesque would resort to again, in very different circumstances.

CHAPTER NINETEEN

The (Very) Long Road to Power

On November 15, 1976, the PQ won power, and René Lévesque, the new MNA for Taillon, became premier of Quebec. From the darkness of the 1970 October Crisis to that glorious day, six short years had passed, but for someone of Lévesque's inordinate lack of patience, it must have seemed a century had gone by. Maybe two.

Obstacle number one on the road to power: Robert Bourassa, whom Lévesque derided as a weakling and Trudeau's pawn. But he proved to be an agile politician. Just a few months after the October Crisis, Bourassa refused to go along with Trudeau's patriation of the Constitution. His was not the most prescient decision, nor was it the wisest, considering the events that followed. Trudeau was livid, of course, but Bourassa calculated that the prime minister's anger would stand him in good stead with the soft nationalists of the province; to be re-elected, he needed Quebec's esteem, not Ottawa's.

Bourassa was as much of a committed social democrat as Lévesque was, and the measures he implemented in that vein, such as legal aid, the granting of the vote to renters in municipal elections, and health insurance for all, earned him the gratitude of voters. On the economic front, his James Bay hydro initiative put him miles ahead of the PQ, and this on the very turf Lévesque thought he owned. Bourassa may have looked weak in person or in the media, and a lot of people felt like kicking sand in his face, but he was a tough opponent to beat. Of course, this benevolent activity was costing the public purse a lot of money, but then, all governments in Canada were on the same drunken spending spree.

Obstacle number two: Lévesque's own Parti Québécois. It must have felt like herding cats at times. Having insisted on a party freed from moneyed influence, Lévesque ended up with more purity than he had bargained for. In the old days, you could silence party members with promises of favours and discreet financial help. Not in the PQ: Lévesque was surrounded by zealots who could kill themselves working for the Cause with no promises of material rewards, only the prospective satisfaction of quenching their fierce desire for History. They were for real, not just silly idealists you could knock off with a few well-chosen retorts.

For instance, at the 1971 convention, young and turbulent MNA Claude Charron moved that, in an independent Quebec, the whole education system in English would be abolished, pure and simple. Party members were elated. Lévesque put his foot down again: "If the motion passes, get yourself another leader!" Fearing that the pope would leave their church and turn into a hermit, the party faithful, true to their old Catholic culture, reverted to their submissive mode and voted down the resolution. Even though Lévesque won every time he played chicken, he hated it.

Fortunately, there was only one convention a year, but Lévesque also had to deal with his Quebec City caucus regularly. He hated that, too. His seven MNAs were all newcomers to politics, but they had wasted no time in behaving like members of a select club and enjoying the pay, the respect, the perks, and the responsibilities of elected officials. Like all other members of the PQ, they adored their leader and wanted to have him in Quebec City more often, to give them guidance, lend them his magic touch for words. But Lévesque would have none of that. Not being a member of the Assembly, he saw no reason to leave his beloved Montreal and waste his precious time in provincial Quebec City. Often rebuffed and left to its own devices, the caucus started to act like an orphaned adult and to make decisions that were sure to displease the founding father. But how else could they get his attention?

Things got rough when MNA Robert Burns, a former union lawyer, decided that the PQ would support workers striking at *La Presse* in the fall of 1971. "The PQ has to be on the side of the workers and the exploited!" he claimed. Lévesque was mad as hell. The last thing he wanted was for the PQ to look as if it were in bed with the unions; the PQ had to remain above the fray, independent! And Lévesque had taken so many pains to build the party's respectability, the second last thing he wanted was to scare conservative-minded and union-hating burghers. Leftist rhetoric, he felt, was bad for credit. He finally managed to rein in Burns, but the episode left bitter memories within the caucus.

Thank goodness there was some good news from time to time. In the 1972 federal election, Pierre Trudeau had very nearly lost power and was now hanging on to his minority government. At least that kept him out of mischief. And the PQ was getting more respectable by the day. Back in 1969, one of Quebec's rare economists with solid government credentials, Jacques Parizeau, had joined the party. He had been followed in 1972 by Claude Morin, a bona fide academic and civil service mandarin who had played an important role in Lesage's Quiet Revolution. Lévesque made another nice catch: Yves Michaud, a personal friend and former journalist and MNA who had made his mark in the Quebec public service under Bourassa. Lévesque was happy, for he knew he needed all the help he could get. An election was looming. The date was set for October 29, 1973.

Ever anxious to establish its economic credibility, the PQ went into battle armed with what was called the Year One Budget. It was to be the first budget of an independent Quebec, and it had been crafted by the PQ's resident thinkers. Jacques Parizeau was shanghaied into defending it. He detested the mission but went ahead anyway, as any good soldier would. Despite his considerable debating skills, Parizeau did not do a very good job on television or on the hustings. The Year One Budget was too inviting a target for fearmongers and even moderate, commonsensical objectors. The rest of the PQ platform was picked apart and roundly criticized from all sides. "What else did you say? An independent Quebec would leave NATO, NORAD? And what about sovereignty-association, where did that go?"

It was a rout worse than anyone had imagined. Bourassa elected 102 members, leaving only 6 PQ MNAs and 2 Social Crediters, who, being of the "Elvis Is Alive" variety, would provide the National Assembly with much-needed comic relief in the years to come. By way of consolation, the PQ had increased its share of the popular vote from 23 percent to 35 percent, but it had little to show for it. Camille Laurin and another PQ MNA had bitten the dust. Even Lévesque had been defeated again. The only consolation was the election of Jacques-Yvan Morin, a law professor with gravitas to spare.

That night, as spirits were sagging among the party faithful, Lévesque again played the reassuring father figure. He reminded everyone in the audience that barely a year before, Nixon, too, had been re-elected with an obese majority only to find himself mired in the Watergate scandal. "So, patience, my friends, patience.... Tonight's disastrous results might just be the harbinger of electoral success...." Again, the magic words had the desired effect: people went home, some of them weeping, just as they did in 1970. No incident, nothing, just a colossal hangover the next day and the prospect of four more arid years in opposition. But at least the PQ was on the ascent.

ONE PARTY MEMBER who was not at all discouraged was Yves Michaud. On the very night of the defeat, he said to Lévesque, "Why don't we start a newspaper that would be solely devoted to the promotion of the independence of Quebec?" Lévesque and his close advisers were enthusiastic. It would be an *indépendantiste* newspaper, the PQ's answer to the federalist *Le Devoir,* then headed by Claude Ryan.

It was a lovely idea but a terrible one. Long gone were the glorious days when political parties owned newspapers that brought money to their coffers while ministering to the faithful. Launched on February 28, 1974, and called *Le Jour,* it was a financial as well as an ideological disaster from day one. Once the novelty had worn off, advertisers did not exactly besiege the paper, largely because of its distribution problems; money got tight, and the enthusiastic circulation of the early days melted like snow in April. The newsroom was soon packed with Torquemada-type journalists more interested in Marxist purity than in newsworthy items. Although he was the editor, Yves Michaud lost control of the place; the few good writers he had just walked away in disgust, their pockets empty. *Le Jour* made only one person truly happy: Pierre Bourgault, who panned it with the feral glee of a jilted lover in an eloquent op-ed piece published in ... *Le Devoir.* That proved to be the last nail in the coffin. The adventure ended in August 1976.

In a strange, roundabout way, *Le Jour* served its purpose in that its demise led Premier Bourassa to believe that he could now score an easy one in the PQ's empty net. He would be telling the voters: Look, these fellows can't even run a newspaper, and now they want to manage the province, even a country? Come on.... Bourassa could have stayed comfortably in power for one more year, but the *Le Jour* debacle gave him too tempting a target. Going after the PQ proved, however, to be a gross miscalculation.

In what seemed to be more bad news, Pierre Trudeau had been re-elected with a sound majority in July 1974, and his main rivals had all cleared out: Tory Robert Stanfield, replaced by gaffe-prone Joe Clark; the NDP's David Lewis, replaced by the untested Ed Broadbent; and finance minister and perennial challenger John Turner, replaced by no one. Trudeau seemed invincible.

FINALLY, something good happened. The 1973 defeat had been so resounding that even diehard *indépendantistes* were beginning to harbour doubts about their strategy, which was to proclaim Quebec's independence the day after a provincial election. This had scared away a lot of voters. So long as this policy was in place, Premier Bourassa thought that Quebecers would have no choice but to vote for him forever. But voters were not happy with that: they hated feeling captive, and they did not want a government that felt entitled to do whatever it pleased just because re-election was assured for the next century or so.

Enter Claude Morin, the former mandarin who had gone back to teaching. It was he who suggested to Lévesque that, in so many words: "Maybe we could proceed differently … You know … I just had this idea … Maybe we could just run on a good government platform, promise to rid Quebecers of the arrogant and scandal-prone Liberals, and once we have established our credentials as prudent managers, we could hold a referendum on the future of Quebec. Ask voters whether they would agree to go a step further. We would first negotiate a new modus vivendi with Canada and then, slowly but surely, inch our way toward independence, with the Québécois' consent every step of the way. Just a thought …"

Lévesque was enthralled: power first and then a referendum. The politician in him saw all the advantages of this incremental approach and no downside whatsoever. But the same politician also stopped him from making the leap too early. He basically said to Morin, "Go out there, float the idea, talk to the rank-and-file, and if they balk, I'll throw my prestige in the balance and we will get everybody on board." Morin obliged, and it proved to be a wise course of action. With his lengthy experience as a senior civil servant, his good-parishioner looks, and his fatherly pipe, Morin was the man for the job. His speaking style was soothing, never confrontational, although he could be counted on to silence the babbling dreamers in the PQ with a well-placed barb. He could even knock off Pierre Bourgault with an adroit jab—which he sometimes did—but without alienating the faithful. A rare talent.

As planned, the party members endorsed Morin's gradualist approach, and Lévesque let it be known that he was all for it. Good government first, followed by a referendum, became the creed of the day.

Overnight, the PQ became a lot less scary. It was even attracting new and interesting members: young Pierre Marc Johnson for instance, a medical doctor as well as a lawyer and the son of now-deceased UN premier Daniel Johnson. Things looked good, but the caucus was getting restless again. Young Claude Charron was openly critical of Lévesque's absence from Quebec City; firebrand Robert Burns was wondering publicly about Lévesque's *indépendantiste* convictions and was not shy about telling the boss himself: "Listen, if you care so much about this or that issue, get elected first, then we'll discuss it." Lévesque's position suddenly looked shaky; a bruising confrontation was imminent.

Politics is a game in which your opponent's miscalculations make you look like a strategic and tactical genius. The

1976 Summer Olympics had just taken place, and although Montrealers ended up with an Olympic-sized deficit as well as shoddy facilities built in haste (with the unions and contractors lining their pockets and leaving idle cranes to mar the scenery during the events), the public mood was good. It was then that Bourassa decided to gamble. A snap election was called for November 15, 1976, and it inadvertently helped Lévesque avert the showdown with his caucus.

CHAPTER TWENTY

The Do-Gooders

The election results were so good that even René Lévesque was voted in with a comfortable majority in his riding of Taillon, and so were all the other PQ star candidates: perennial foot soldiers like Jacques Parizeau and Bernard Landry, TV talk-show host Lise Payette and Pierre Marc Johnson. Even Camille Laurin was re-elected. Both left-wingers and right-wingers within the PQ were elected. The Liberals had to content themselves with anglophone and French bourgeois ridings. Even Bourassa had gone down in defeat, and the premier resigned as Liberal leader that same night. The UN had come back from limbo but was headed by a non-entity. The same two Social Crediters, who had each switched to a different but losing party, were still there, at least for the laughs.

On election night, addressing a crowd drowning in tears of national joy, Lévesque then summarized: "We are not a little nation, we may indeed be something akin to a great nation. And never in my life have I felt so proud to be a Québécois!" The crowd roared its approval. Promising times were ahead.

The PQ scored early on the social front. The first law they passed was an ethics code for ministers, who were now forbidden from owning any stock in a publicly traded company and had to declare all other business interests. Another act, passed in March 1977, required transparency in political donations. The funding rules governing the PQ would apply to all parties. Electoral mores were to be cleansed forever. Thirty years later virtually all other jurisdictions in Canada have followed suit.

It was also in 1977 that the PQ government passed a law making automobile insurance mandatory and publicly managed, an idea inspired by the NDP in Manitoba, although that fact was seldom mentioned, *naturellement*. The bill was shepherded by Minister Lise Payette, who had considerable trouble convincing her colleagues that state-owned car insurance was the way to go, especially in a province where one motorist out of five had no insurance whatsoever. But thanks to Lévesque's support, Payette won the day.

BILL 101 was another landmark piece of legislation, although the ride this time was much rougher. Camille Laurin, minister of cultural development, played the starring role. Supported by a cast of nationalist ideologues with impeccable credentials, he first authored a white paper on the subject of language legislation. From now on, French would be the language of work in Quebec; all businesses with more than fifty employees would have to function in French; immigrants would be schooled in French only; French would be the dominant language in any kind of advertising or public announcement; and section 133 of the British North America (BNA) Act, regarding the language to be used in the National Assembly and in courts, would be trumped by section 1 of the language bill. The Cabinet liked it; Laurin was beaming.

There was only one problem: Lévesque had very strong reservations. To him, it was the kind of problem that would solve itself with the independence of Quebec. The fact that the government would have to legislate in linguistic matters he found "humiliating." So he dragged his feet, as he had earlier with the reform of Quebec's education system. But Laurin felt he had history on his side: the French language, after all, was very much the creation of the French state. It was through legislation and the heavy hand of the state that regional dialects like Alsatian, Breton, and Occitan had been all but wiped out; it was through legislation and regulations that French had really become France's national language. Therefore, it was only natural for the state of Quebec to use all its powers to impose the language of the majority of Quebecers. We may not be the masters of our economic house, reasoned Laurin, but at least with this bill, no employer will ever have the authority to force its employees to speak English among themselves. Linguistically speaking, Quebecers would finally be at home in their own province. Lévesque countered that such legislation would stimulate the then ongoing exodus of anglophones, and he was right in that respect: from 1976 to 1981, 130,000 Anglo Quebecers left the province, taking with them their diplomas, their expertise, their bank accounts. It was quite the bloodletting. But Laurin would not be budged.

The expected furor erupted with the tabling of Bill 101. Claude Ryan of *Le Devoir* excoriated the government, and the English press was up in arms. For many anglophones, Bill 101 was indeed the writing on the wall: they had to leave. But the PQ government thankfully held its own. Yes, thankfully.

A few years later, with the dominance of the French language, Quebec had become a very distinct society in Canada. Good heavens, you could even order in French in a restaurant in Chinatown! And the mythical saleslady yelling "Speak white" to Québécois customers at Eaton's had vanished from sight. False memories of her remained only as a badge of honour for militant nationalists who would invoke that urban legend to gain hero status with disbelieving young people later accustomed to a French-only Quebec.

The passing of Bill 101 marked a victory for the PQ, but with dubious consequences. More and more Québécois felt increasingly secure about the future of their language. And with the weakening of age-old nativist insecurity, the need for an independent Quebec became less acute. All his life, René Lévesque had wanted Quebecers to feel confident about themselves; now they felt so confident they no longer felt the urge to separate: a classic case of the law of unintended consequences at work.

THINGS MAY HAVE BEEN GOING WELL on the social front, but on the economic front, it was a different matter.

Like their Liberal forebears of the Quiet Revolution, PQ politicians remained convinced that the state must be the visible hand of the economy. They wanted the government to be front and centre in all economic matters, and Finance Minister Jacques Parizeau was only too happy to oblige. Hence a flurry of regulations and subsidies designed to boost industrial and commercial activity. Some did the job, but others simply did not work at all. And the economy

sometimes simply refused to co-operate. As French politician Pierre Mendès France once famously said about
hyperactive interventionism: "Sometimes, the economy gets
even." It got even in Quebec. When the PQ took power in
1976, unemployment stood at 8.5 percent, and it had
reached 15.9 percent when they were ousted by the Liberals
in 1985.

Parizeau's *ne-pas-laisser-faire* stance was compounded by
the influence of the PQ's left wing. In the 1960s and early
1970s, a number of MNAs had been enamoured with the
socialist theories in vogue in countries where they had never
set foot, which was probably why they loved them so. They
were keen to import those abstract models and make them
work here.

One good example of that trend was Tricofil, a textile mill
in the Laurentians where sons had succeeded fathers for
generations at the hiring office. In 1974, business being bad
and the owners having decided to fold, the workers had
bought the mill from them, but it had proven to be a rough
venture. Of course, their cause proved irresistible to the
intellectual bourgeoisie of the time and the PQ left wing. In
1977, when the worker entrepreneurs went to Quebec City
cap in hand to get help—to the tune of $724,000—they
were greeted with sympathy. The response was less enthusi-

astic in 1978 when they went back to the well, this time for a $1.25 million bailout. The company went belly up in 1982.

But the PQ was far from done with expensive utopia. Asbestos was their biggest target, a costly mix of emotional economics and political mythology. The desire to control the province's natural resources was still very much in the air, and the repression of asbestos miners under Duplessis was now the stuff of legend and literature. The nationalization of the asbestos mines was to be a sweet revenge on the past as well as a masterful stroke of planning for the future. Quebec's underbelly held the greatest asbestos reserves in the world. René Lévesque, never at a loss for foreign inspiration, even boasted, "We are the Arabs of asbestos"—and nobody had laughed. Soon after gaining power, the PQ proceeded to expropriate General Dynamics, the American owners of Asbestos Mining. The company balked, and its owners were silenced with buckets full of money. After several months of bickering and negotiation, the final price tag for the govern- ment of Quebec was $435 million (in 1978 dollars). No problem, said the PQ, asbestos would be a second Hydro-Québec.

The Quebec government lost every penny of its invest-ment. At the time the deal was closed, asbestos was already being denounced as a health hazard, and its use would eventually be banned in industrialized countries. The real business of the future would be the removal of asbestos from buildings. Thirty years after the nationalization of asbestos, all that is left of the PQ dream are unemployed men ill with asbestos-induced cancer and vast expanses of landscape ravaged by years of strip mining.

THE PQ GOVERNMENT was also unlucky in its dealings with Wall Street. But here the lion's share of the blame lies at Lévesque's feet. Soon after the PQ was elected, American financiers, usually oblivious to events above their northern border, got curious about Quebec. Lévesque was then invited to address the prestigious Economic Club in New York. He was eager to go. It would be his first official foray abroad, and he desperately wanted to reassure Big American Money about Quebec's peaceful intentions. So down he went to the Big Apple, made his speech, bombed, and rushed back home, furious.

What happened? Well, he tried to please his audience by telling them that Quebec was engaged in a course similar to the movement that had led the Thirteen Colonies to the Declaration of Independence in 1776. No one was flattered. Lévesque loved to pepper his speeches with foreign comparisons. It pleased his audiences mightily at home. Not abroad. In fact, he reminded his listeners more of Jefferson Davis and the six hundred thousand people who were butchered in the Civil War. And none of the reassurances he gave stuck. Resorting again to dubious historical references, he blamed the coolness of the reception on the presence in the audience of a "phalanx" of Canadian businessmen, a "fifth column." This did not ring true: there was nothing Roman or Nazi about what had happened. Lévesque only managed to draw more hoots of laughter. In his memoirs, adolescent as ever in refusing to take responsibility, he blamed his public servants for the poor quality of the speech; he also wrote that he was not at ease in the *de rigueur* tuxedo.

But that was how heartbroken he was. He had wanted badly to shine in the United States and failed miserably. While some leading Quebec nationalists of his generation looked to France for the compensatory promised land that would heal their inferiority complex, Lévesque had no time for the French. Wine was all he liked about them, and maybe their films and pretty women. He found them pompous, patronizing, tight-assed; he did not even feel grateful for their signs of interest. When he was awarded the Légion d'honneur by French president Giscard d'Estaing, all he could do was wince in embarrassment. And like every other nationalist, he was impatient with the repeated French expressions of gratitude to Canada for Vimy, Dieppe, and Juno Beach. To him, France remained the weak country defeated by Germany and the Vietminh; it was also the imperial power that had denied independence to Algeria at the cost of hundreds of thousands of lives.

Lévesque dreamed of Liz Taylor, not Brigitte Bardot. Which explains why in all of his sorties to the United States over the course of his nine years as premier, his failure to seduce his hard-nosed audiences was all the more painful. And yet, Lévesque was so proud of having served in an American uniform. He said countless times that, next to Quebec, America was the country he loved most. Like so many other Québécois, he spent every summer vacation on the beaches of New England. Whereas Canada was to him a bland monolith unworthy of his interest, America was God's gift to the world.

In fact, his behaviour was typical of many nationalists who found something redeeming about the loud adoration of all things American: in extolling their North American-ness, they accentuated their estrangement from Canada, and it somehow put a balm on the self-loathing they felt for not yet having made their nation a country. They also intuited, somewhat perversely, that their *américanité* would enhance their profile in America-mad France. It was a very bizarre case of geopolitics coming to the rescue of a weak neo-colonial psyche.

But it was all wishful thinking. Like sovereignty-association. Which leads us, of course, to the May 20, 1980, referendum.

CHAPTER TWENTY-ONE

Failure

It was a lost cause from the start, but a gamble Lévesque just could not resist.

The passing of the enabling referendum legislation had stirred quite a debate, with the government pollsters constantly gauging the population's appetite for independence. What was clear from day one, and remained crystal clear, was that Quebecers would vote overwhelmingly No to a clear question such as "Do you agree to separate from Canada and form a new country called Quebec?" So what to do? The PQ in opposition had promised a referendum, and it felt it had to go to the people at least once. All right, but what would the question look like? At first, many in the PQ wanted a frank, mature question such as the one above, but when it came to formulating it, the courage to use lucid terms seemed to desert even the boldest. Nobody wanted No for an answer.

Based on the pollsters' findings, on October 10, 1978, in the National Assembly, Lévesque formulated the PQ's referendum position: "Our intention is not to achieve sovereignty first and then negotiate an association with Canada. We do not want to break up Canada, only change radically our relationship with the rest of Canada. Sovereignty and association will therefore be achieved concurrently, without any breaking-up."

Even within the PQ, Lévesque's objective, and the process he put forward to attain it, continued to raise serious doubts, especially among former RIN members. They wanted independence and nothing but. The Liberal opposition was of course more blunt in its criticism. "So Quebec will go it alone, but what will Canada say? Who says it will go along?" As usual, Lévesque dismissed such questions as "details," and many started to believe, as he did, that faced with a clear majority of Yes voters, Canada would have no choice but to negotiate a new governing compact.

Then something strange occurred. The constant talk of sovereignty-association caused a process of self-hypnosis to set in. The Péquistes were applying to politics Pascal's famous advice on how to believe in God: "You only need to pray, and with the act of praying, faith will come." Sovereignty-association became an act of faith, a technique familiar to a place that had been staunchly Catholic for so long. All you had to do was to repeat the words often enough and the belief would come. And it did: to many, anyway.

The next question was when. The PQ government had been caught up with Bill 101 and a host of important social measures during their first two years in office. In 1979 the situation had cleared up a bit. People were, in general, satisfied with the PQ government, which had managed to remain as clean as a whistle. The only scandal had been caused by Lévesque himself, of all people. On February 5, 1977, driving home from a soiree at Yves Michaud's, Lévesque had run over and killed an old homeless man who had added a dangerous twist to his panhandling technique: he would lie in the streets in the hope of eliciting more compassion. The police had charged Lévesque only for his failure to wear glasses while driving, as he was required to do according to his driver's licence (not wearing his glasses was an adolescent vanity typical of the man). That was it. Lévesque had gotten off scot-free, and people quickly forgot all about it.

In April 1979, the government further clarified its objectives by releasing a white paper on the sovereignty-association project: a monetary union with Canada, a common tariffs policy, the sharing of the debt, guarantees for minorities. Everything was there. But it failed to arouse any enthusiasm. Diehard separatists, who no longer dared speak their name, were not happy with the Canadian connection, and soft nationalists seemed to remain skeptical.

The economy was not exactly buoyant, but there were no major signs of a weakening. Signals of hope came, of all places, from Ottawa. In the federal election of May 1979, Pierre Trudeau was beaten by young Progressive Conservative leader Joe Clark. Clark would head a minority government. Trudeau seemed to be on the way out, and indeed he resigned as leader of the Liberals in November. Not only was Lévesque finally rid of Trudeau, Clark had also promised foolishly not to get involved in any Quebec referendum. This would be an *entre nous* affair. To top it all off, one of Clark's influential ministers, David Crombie, had said publicly that the federal government would be crazy not to negotiate with the Quebec government in the aftermath of a Yes vote. So things were starting to look good.

Lévesque also saw another unwitting ally in the new leader of the provincial Liberals, Claude Ryan, who had been on the job only a year. But inexperience was not his problem. Au contraire, he may have had too much of it. Ryan had been the pontificating publisher of *Le Devoir* for a very long time; he was a man set in his ways who would not make any concession to the game of politics. For years, he had written his political oracles in the comfort of his office with no obligation to please anyone. He was admired for the cold, businesslike logic he brought to his weekly analysis of current events as well as for his sharp style, qualities that were very Trudeau-like in a way. However, the man was about as charismatic as an eggplant. When the Liberals had approached him to replace Robert Bourassa, he had initially turned them down for personal reasons: his wife was not well, and he did not want to leave her side. Unfortunately for him and them, doctors gave Madeleine Ryan a clean bill of health, and he reconsidered. He had finally agreed to let himself be anointed Liberal leader after a token contest, and he had taken over with a sense of moral superiority that was sure to turn off even his warmest supporters. The new Liberal leader was in the position of the suave and respected hockey analyst who agrees one day to coach in the NHL. Problem was, Quebecers knew their hockey and could boo any coach out of town.

Blessed with opponents like Clark and Ryan, Lévesque felt he could make a go of it. The only remaining problem was the question itself. Lévesque's advisers and pollsters consulted the best minds around them and ended up submitting to Cabinet a very long question, a sixty-five-word sentence, in fact. For two exhausting days, ministers and lawyers juggled with it, trying to improve it. But their painful effort only revealed how gripped they were by anguish and doubt. "A swampy question," said playwright

Michel Tremblay later, confirming Talleyrand's musings about the power of self-confidence: "If you know you are right, you do not need to write forty-five pages about it." Lévesque and his people must have sensed somewhere, somehow, that they were on the wrong side of history.

The question was tabled in the National Assembly on December 12, 1979. Having for once paid heed to his image-makers, who had found him a nice suit with the right tie, Lévesque delivered a masterful speech. Claude Ryan's response was timid, fumbling, pathetic. In the following days, polls showed a positive response. All of a sudden, the referendum gamble looked very winnable.

But things had already started to go wrong. The very day before, December 11, Joe Clark's government had been toppled in the House of Commons over a budget that was absurdly impolitic. Trudeau had agreed to come out of retirement to have another bout with Clark. The Liberals were easily swept back to power, with a comfortable majority, in February 1980. With Trudeau back in the game, having won seventy-four of the seventy-five seats in Quebec, federalists in Quebec, who had sixty-five-word-long questions about Ryan as their leader, sighed with relief. The great showdown between Pierre and René would take place on May 20, 1980.

The referendum campaign started officially on April 15. The Yes camp, headed by Premier Lévesque, made two major mistakes. Lise Payette, the former popular TV star and the only major feminine presence in Cabinet, made some casual remarks at a PQ meeting about Yvette, the mythical little girl of the school readers published by Quebec's education ministry: the good girl who washes the dishes with her mother and learns sewing and needlework while the boys take out the garbage and play hockey in the backyard. Payette was right to criticize such an outmoded view of girls and women, but she then added that she hated Claude Ryan because he was married to an "Yvette." The following day, the Quebec press crucified Payette for having insulted Madeleine Ryan, an accomplished person in her own right. Lévesque thought it was a tempest in a teapot. The teapot proved to be an ocean, with thousands of women showing up at rallies in support of the No side, the Canadian option. The Yes men were unable to muster a credible reply; they looked weak, mauled by some invisible beast and bleeding profusely.

The other mistake was Lévesque's own. At a meeting on May 8, he reminded his listeners that Trudeau's middle name was Elliott, as in "watch out, he is not one of ours." For Lévesque, it was a very rare slip into negative nationalism: exclusion and divisiveness based on blood purity. Until then, the man who had been inside Dachau in 1945 had managed to act as an inclusive sovereignist, as if it had nothing to do with nationalism. Not only had he weakened the nobility of his cause, Lévesque had also stepped on the tiger's tail. And the tiger jumped into the fray thirsting for blood. Six days later, on May 14, Trudeau made a speech at the Paul Sauvé Arena in Montreal that was so impassioned it gave all voters goosebumps. All of a sudden, the emotional appeal was no longer a strictly Quebec thing: it had changed sides and was now Canada's. From there on, it was downhill for the Yes camp.

On May 20, the tally was almost 60 percent for the No side. In his speech that night, Trudeau nobly paid tribute to those who had dared to dream otherwise and toiled so hard for their cause. Ryan played the part of the sore winner: he took all the credit for himself, managing to insult both Yes and No voters. Lévesque, who had been expecting the outcome for days now, was his modest and subdued self, but able as usual to find soothing words for the disappointed faithful. "If I heard you right, you are telling me: until next time!" Spoken like a true leader who may be down but not out, resilient enough to find hope in his pain. He then enjoined the crowd to sing Quebec's unofficial anthem,

"Gens du pays," singing the first bars himself. Tone-deaf as he was, that required real courage. The crowd followed suit but with little heart. It was just too painful. People then calmly dispersed, as they had several times before when history and greatness had eluded them.

Lévesque was never blamed for the loss, his position in the PQ never challenged after the defeat. The only grumbling came from the orthodox wing of the party, chief among them Finance Minister Jacques Parizeau, who resented the lack of boldness in his camp. But he contented himself with *sotto voce* criticism. One Lévesque detractor who was more vocal, as he was wont to be, was Pierre Bourgault. He jubilantly predicted a "Night of the Long Knives" for the inventor of the gradualist approach, Claude Morin.

"Night of the Long Knives" is the phrase history has retained for the very bloody night when the SS got rid of the SA to give Hitler the sole mastery of the Nazi movement. It was a phrase that Lévesque used himself sometimes. He would later find another use for it.

CHAPTER TWENTY-TWO

The Beautiful Loser

Now what if Lévesque had done things differently? Let us leave history for fiction and see how that goes, beginning with his speech of May 20, 1980.

> My dear friends. You have seen the results for yourselves: there should be no doubt in our minds that a strong majority of Quebecers still feel a strong bond to their country of birth or adoption, Canada. We are a democratic nation, and we accept the decision of the Quebec nation. But we did not dream in vain. In our quest for an independent country, we brought beneficial and lasting changes to our society. There may come another day when you will decide to go a step further in the transformation of this land. But now is not the time: another day, maybe. Just like you, I have given my heart and soul to this pursuit, and the time has come for me to step back and let someone else take over. I have just informed the Parti Québécois that

I am stepping down as president; I have also resigned as premier and member for Taillon. All that remains for me to do is to thank you from the bottom of my heart for having accompanied me on this wonderful journey. I know that, together, we have built a more self-confident Quebec, and that self-confidence will endure. Thank you all, and goodbye, my dear, dear friends.

You would have heard a pin drop in the Paul Sauvé Arena. And then the sobs, followed by shouts of No! No!, the only word the crowd had refused to utter during the thirty-five-day campaign. But Lévesque would not have stayed for the show of sorrow; he would have exited quickly and vanished into the night.

The following day, more resignations would have followed: Camille Laurin in the morning, Claude Morin in the afternoon. A few days later, Pierre Marc Johnson would have been anointed PQ president and premier-elect. In the spring of 1981, he would have easily beaten the ungraceful Ryan. Bent on turning the page, Johnson could have negotiated the patriation of the Constitution with Trudeau, and both Quebec and Canada would have entered a new era of compromise and understanding.

As for Lévesque, after a two-month holiday in Provence, he would have resumed his career as a journalist with zeal. In the fall, he would have mesmerized his audiences, both French and English, with his reporting on the American election campaign, when Reagan ejected Carter from the White House. He would have showed them that *he still had it*, that there was not a single cobweb on the rejuvenated broadcaster. After a year or so, he would have become such a fixture on TV with his comments on foreign affairs that people would have forgotten he had once been the leader of a separatist party and premier of Quebec. He would have become René Lévesque again, plain and simple, basking in love and respect.

He would have driven around Montreal in his ordinary car, and people would sometimes have recognized him behind the wheel, gawking for so long they would have forgotten that the light had turned green, a rare occurrence in Quebec. Or he would have been spotted in a subway car with his beautiful wife, Corinne, his long-time companion whom he had married in 1978. People would have stared at him in awe, or sometimes burst into applause, and he would have walked away, wincing and grinning. In restaurants, he would have had a hard time paying for his meals: there would always have been an admirer around to pick up

Monsieur Lévesque's tab, without making a show of it, of course.

His resignation would have revealed his profound political genius. By making the ultimate political sacrifice, he would have unburdened the nationalist family of a dream too heavy to bear and wiped out their shame at having lost. He would have also allowed the PQ to rejuvenate itself and reconnect with its true universal values: justice, equality, progress for all. Paradoxically, his act of humility would have boosted Quebecers' sense of dignity. Quebec would finally have been at peace with itself. Elsewhere in Canada, no one would have dared gloat about the separatists' failure. People would only have said, "Well, they tried, it didn't work, so they moved on, and after that, we all regrouped and forged ahead together as one. Like Wayne Gretzky and Mario Lemieux joining forces to beat the Soviets on the ice."

Few people would have realized that Lévesque's return to a normal life would in fact have been in keeping with a strong tradition in Quebec. Once retired, Maurice Richard, too, was the very symbol of the once mighty who had gone back to a humble life. He had been loved as a player; he was later adored as a man. Another well-known example was Paul-Émile Cardinal Léger, who had resigned his prestigious position as Archbishop of Montreal to work as a missionary in Africa. He had been loved; he was now worshipped. Quebecers, being true democrats, like their heroes to act as ordinary people, like one of them. Humility is their preferred virtue, and they amply reward it with the kind of adoration that is simply inaccessible to the rich, the famous, and the powerful. Lévesque would have finally entered the Quebec pantheon of unassuming heroes and saints.

NONE OF THAT HAPPENED, of course. Instead of walking away into self-imposed exile, wounded and forever beloved, Lévesque chose to stay on, like a gambler bent on recouping his losses.

His descent into hell began that very night, May 20, 1980.

CHAPTER TWENTY-THREE

The Constitutional Drama

Trudeau badly wanted to patriate the Canadian Constitution from Great Britain, so that it could be amended here with the consent of the Canadian people. Canada would then finally excise this embarrassing anomaly from its independence. He also wanted to enrich the Constitution with a Charter of Rights and Freedoms that would protect every citizen against prejudice and arbitrariness. Thanks to the Charter, he reasoned, there would be no more second-class citizens in this country (such as Aboriginals, women, immigrants, and so many others); minority rights would be respected; and the state would never again be able to abuse its powers. It was the very reason he had entered politics; it was the fight of his life. Strengthened by the referendum result, Trudeau had decided to go it alone.

Of course, there were obstacles. First and foremost were the change-averse premiers who feared that the new constitutional order might dilute their powers and prerogatives. Trudeau's only allies were Ontario, then headed by Premier Bill Davis, and New Brunswick, with Dick Hatfield at the helm. Seven provinces were against patriation. Some just wanted to stop Trudeau dead in his tracks, others thought that some form of opposition would produce a better deal for them. So they gathered in the fall of 1980 to plan their strategy against Ottawa.

What about Quebec? The PQ had just lost its referendum and was in no mood to say yes to the prime minister after having just heard a resounding no from the citizenry. Within the Quebec government, only Intergovernmental Affairs Minister Claude Morin wanted to forge an alliance with the seven. To him, it was a win-win proposition: either we derail Trudeau's plans by standing up to him or Quebec gets a better deal out of it. Some ministers, like Jacques Parizeau in Finance, were dead set against any move on the constitutional front. Their reasoning went something like this: "If Trudeau wants his constitution, let him have it. If we sit on our hands, we will not have to acknowledge it and that will give us a free hand in the future. And if Trudeau fails, well, we'll be even." Anyway, an election was looming in Quebec, so Morin was told to remain in touch with the seven and to tread carefully, which he did.

Any government looks tired after four years in power, so the PQ was not doing well in the polls. Then, as winter set in, its fortunes seemed to pick up. Quebecers had had ample opportunity to have a second look at Claude Ryan, and they did not like what they saw: an authoritarian man, a cold fish with frighteningly outdated morals whose platform was as dull as dishwater. Then Lévesque promised there would be no referendum if he was re-elected. That changed a lot of things. Overnight, the government's satisfaction index went up, and people felt more comfortable with the idea of the PQ remaining in power. The party was doing all right.

It was not much of a contest: on April 13, 1981, the PQ was returned to power with an even larger majority—eighty seats—and Ryan was soon in trouble within the QLP. So there was some fairness in life after all. Lévesque could now turn his attention to Ottawa. And Trudeau.

In the spring of 1981, acting on instructions from the re-elected PQ government, Morin negotiated an accord with the seven dissenting provinces. The now Gang of Eight agreed on the following: no Charter of Rights, no veto for any province, and opting-out for all, which meant that if Ottawa wanted to indulge in some social spending, the provinces would be free to take the money and go it alone. Lévesque approved the accord without even referring it to the National Assembly. Not everybody was happy, of course, for it was thanks to the veto that Quebec had twice managed to block Ottawa's constitutional manoeuvres. But Lévesque was so convinced that Trudeau's scheme would fail anyway that he did not mind betting the house and the barn on the whole strategy.

Also in the spring of 1981, Lévesque attended the first round of discussions in Ottawa as a full-fledged member of the Gang of Eight, and events seemed to confirm Morin's optimistic prognosis. Right in the middle of the talks, a leaked federal document revealed that Ottawa was less than forthcoming about its strategy: it had programmed deadlock from the start in order to justify unilateral patriation. The premiers were understandably furious, and the talks came to a bitter end. But Lévesque was all smiles. Trudeau had failed and was booed for his sneaky approach. Round one to Lévesque.

Then the Supreme Court of Canada handed down its decision on whether unilateral action by Ottawa was legal. The court said yes, it was legal, but it would be contrary to convention if Ottawa went ahead. Immediately, Lévesque had a motion passed by the National Assembly, with Ryan's support, to condemn Ottawa's unilateralism. The aim here was to unite the Québécois family and intimidate Trudeau into inaction. Lévesque had won round two easily. The knockout punch was nearing.

Then came the November federal-provincial talks. This time, Lévesque should have heeded Parizeau's advice and stayed home, but the card-player in him found the temptation irresistible. He went to Ottawa accompanied by Marc-André Bédard, his Attorney General; Claude Morin, his usual negotiator; and Claude Charron, the youthful House leader who had quite a flair for strategy. The Gang of Eight still looked solid, but Lévesque was beginning to have doubts, he said later. The aim of the Quebec delegation was simply to let the talks drag on, then declare deadlock and full victory, and go home. It was to be a short stay in Ottawa.

As the talks seemed to be heading nowhere, Ottawa made a spectacular move. On the morning of November 4, Trudeau proposed a deal to Lévesque: the premier of Quebec would support patriation and the Charter on the condition that a referendum on the process would be held in the next six months. Lévesque reacted with stupefying swiftness: he agreed! All observers present were stunned, especially the Quebec media contingent: What? Ottawa and Quebec would make a deal? The old foes Trudeau and Lévesque would now be allies? Now that was unexpected. It was as if the pope had suddenly joined the Orange Lodge.

Charron was in for a major surprise when he gave his gleeful account of the morning's discussions to the Quebec press. Summing up what had happened, Lise Bissonnette, the *grande dame* of *Le Devoir,* who was not normally given to coarse language, echoed Charron's enthusiasm: "So, basically, you got Trudeau by the short and curlies." Charron took the comment as a compliment and as a blessing for Quebec's course of action.

Now why in heaven's name had Lévesque agreed to Trudeau's proposal? Well, it was, again, a gamble he was sure to win. But there was more to it. Patriation was not a big deal for Lévesque; his profound disinterest in constitutional matters was something he made no secret of. The Charter, though, was a different kettle of fish. This was where he and Trudeau parted ways irrevocably. As a convinced nationalist, Lévesque was dead set against any constitutional provision that could override the will of the legislature. In his political vision of the world, the will of the nation as expressed in the makeup of the legislature was to rule supreme, and he was sure that Quebecers would vote massively against Canada's Charter in order to protect the supremacy of the nation. Trudeau believed precisely the opposite: in his political vision of the world, the rule of law was based on the individual, and no legislature would be allowed to trample the rights of any citizen. Next to the Charter, even patriation was no big deal for him. But he wanted both so badly that no one was surprised to see him make a deal with the devil himself in order to achieve his purpose. So, round three to Lévesque?

In the afternoon, Trudeau handed the premiers the draft of the proposal made to Quebec in the morning. It said that all provinces would have to sign on to the agreement; all of them would also have to agree to patriation, the Charter, and the amending formula (any future constitutional amendment would require the consent of seven provinces that together represented at least 50 percent of the population); and finally, all provinces would have to hold a referendum within ten months of the patriation. Lévesque balked: that was not the horse he had bought in the morning. After leaving the conference for the night, he said that Ottawa's proposal sounded like "Chinese" to him. He went back to his hotel in Hull, where a moose dinner awaited him. He felt there was still time to devise another strategy.

But some people who stayed in Ottawa got busy, very busy. Most notably the two Roys, Roy McMurtry, the Attorney General of Ontario, and his counterpart from Saskatchewan, Roy Romanow. The general feeling was that, since Lévesque had broken with the Gang of Eight in agreeing with Trudeau, there was no more Gang of Eight. Everyone was on his own again, everything was back on the table, and all participants were afforded a new start. In the course of the night, an accord was struck between the majority of the provinces and the federal government. Only Manitoba did not sign on. The draft that was submitted to the premiers at breakfast the following day said basically this: patriation would take place, the Charter would be incorporated in the new Constitution, and any future constitutional amendment would require the consent of seven provinces representing at least 50 percent of the population. However, the deal would include a notwithstanding clause, valid for five years only, which any province could invoke in the event that it did not agree with an amendment to the Charter. But the clause would not apply to cases dealing with minority language education where student numbers warranted it.

Lévesque was floored. The whole card game had changed overnight: the players at the table had switched sides; the stakes had changed; and Lévesque could not even get a cash-out because the currency had changed. He was left with nothing, and he had no fallback position. The only choice he had was to walk away or sign—and sign he could not.

Jean Chrétien, the federal justice minister, who had been the chief negotiator for Ottawa throughout and who was in the breakfast room that morning, saw a Lévesque more distraught than ever: a man, he said, who looked like the father who had gambled away his paycheque and faced the prospect of returning home empty-handed.

The Quebec premier's first reaction was to walk out and take the first plane home. Fortunately for him, Charron was at his side and implored him to stay. "Okay, they got a new deal," he told Lévesque, "but you can't leave in a huff now like a sore loser. That would look real bad. You have to stay to the end to show that you have been betrayed. Furthermore, the stalemate between Quebec and Ottawa will endure, and that's what we want." Lévesque took his advice, stayed until the end, and departed with bitter words for the other, jubilant first ministers.

CHAPTER TWENTY-FOUR

Trouble

Quebec's reaction was predictable. In political spheres, shock was quickly followed by outrage. With the support of Claude Ryan, who had never agreed with Trudeau on anything, the National Assembly passed a motion condemning the new constitutional deal; the nationalist family was again united; Trudeau was reviled; and Canada was portrayed as a foreign country bent on imposing its will on Quebec. As for Lévesque, the usual malcontents berated him publicly for having played his hand badly. But in general people accepted his version of events: Big Bad Canada had stabbed Honest Quebec in the back. Within the PQ, there was criticism of the leader, but it was largely muted. Nobody dared to blame the founding father; his hurt gaze silenced any reproach.

With the French-speaking Quebec press siding almost unanimously with Lévesque, the phrase "Night of the Long Knives" took root in Quebec's political vocabulary, even though there could be no similarity between the events in Ottawa and the Nazis' murderous fest. But the words stuck: another manifestation of the colonized imagination of the time, which today still grips the minds of Quebec's intellectual elite. The whole episode became an article of faith: poor, straight-shooting René Lévesque had been betrayed by another Québécois—mean, nasty Pierre Trudeau—and all of English Canada had ganged up on him afterwards. Defeat and underhandedness had restored Lévesque's political virginity, so much so that he was now untouchable. In that sense, Trudeau's constitutional victory resulted in a political victory for Lévesque, the new hero-victim of Quebec. Also, in a perverse way, Canada's triumph morphed into a major political advantage for the province: from then on, under the aegis of politicians of all stripes, Quebec would consider itself the victim state par excellence. Of course, this was a phony posture, but one that could be milked forever. The 1981 constitutional drama, the saddest chapter of Lévesque's political legend, became the gift that keeps on giving. Nationalist mythology benefited immensely, because grievance is the indispensable glue of minority identity. The Acadians had their Deportation, the Métis had Louis Riel, Quebec would now have the "Night of the Long Knives." Not a bad deal at all, come to think of it.

And nobody, but nobody, remarked on the fact that Lévesque and his entourage had in fact organized their own constitutional deadlock with Ottawa. As Marc-André

Bédard, Lévesque's Attorney General, had said, "If we end up making a deal with Ottawa, how are we going to explain that to our rank-and-file members?" For the PQ to succeed, constitutional talks had to fail, but they had not, and Trudeau was to blame because he had walked away from the poker game with the pot.

The only problem was that the general population was not as disgusted as Lévesque and the PQ strategists had hoped. Many felt sorry for Lévesque. And as happened within the PQ, there was not a word of reproach for the family man who had squandered his paycheque at the casino. People found it more convenient to blame the casino instead. Somehow, the Québécois liked his melodrama. But their sympathy did not take them to the streets in protest, and in general, their reaction was muted. After all, the whole business about the Constitution and the Charter sounded too arcane to most—not worth a demonstration or a riot.

The only ones who were jubilant after the Ottawa debacle were the hardliners within the PQ and outside. They harped on endlessly about the rejection of Quebec, and they finally had all the evidence in the world to prove to the skeptics that Canada did not really want them around. Negative emotions regarding Canada had crystallized. And for a while, it seemed that Lévesque would radicalize his stance and show more boldness in his approach.

Meanwhile, Lévesque was actually going through a private drama that nobody suspected: he had been informed that Claude Morin, his trusted minister of intergovernmental affairs in charge of all the negotiations with Ottawa, had been on the RCMP payroll until 1977 as an informant. Morin tried to justify himself by telling Lévesque that he was the one who, in fact, had infiltrated the federal secret police; he had taken no money for himself, and he had donated the dubious proceeds to his church. Still, the optics were so bad that Lévesque had no choice but to force his minister to resign. All of this was done in secrecy, practically no one knew about this whole affair, and Lévesque was alone with his acute feeling of betrayal. He eventually forgave Morin, but he was weakened. From then on, the gradualist approach would be dead in the water.

At the PQ's National Council in the fall of 1981, Lévesque, oozing anger, lashed out at the federal government. The party faithful were easily convinced that the PQ was now on the way to a complete break with Canada. And then, at the party's general convention in early December, the membership passed two radical resolutions, one discarding forever the concept of association with Canada and another saying that Quebec could become a sovereign state without the support of the majority of the population. But Lévesque realized he had gone too far when he saw the membership applaud the entry of Jacques Rose, a member of the FLQ cell that had caused "the death of Pierre Laporte"; it rankled him even more when he heard party members hail Rose as one of their "pioneers." Pierre Bourgault and the radicals in the PQ were smiling again.

Lévesque had had enough. He immediately disallowed both resolutions and let it be known that he was having second thoughts about his future within the PQ. Again, the old game of brinkmanship worked its magic. A few days later, the fever within the PQ having abated, the party elders came up with a face-saving gimmick for all: the party would hold a referendum in early 1982 disallowing both resolutions and reinstituting the concept of association. Quickly dubbed the "renérendum," the consultation worked out well for Lévesque, with 95 percent of the membership voting for his position. There was a slight problem, however: only half of the members had bothered to vote. That and the overwhelming vote of approval, reminiscent of the kind of electoral scores common in the Communist dictatorships of the time, made the whole exercise look suspicious. Lévesque the democrat all of a sudden looked like an autocrat. But he could not have cared less. He had regained mastery of his party, he was now safe in the saddle again.

Lévesque's hard luck seemed to persist. In February 1982, minister Claude Charron had to resign after pleading guilty to a charge of shoplifting. He had gone shopping at Eaton's and had walked away with a jacket. He had been caught fleeing by security guards and was recognized by them as "Claude Charron, the PQ minister." Charron had thought for a while that Eaton's would not press charges, but the company went ahead. It all looked so bad. Here was a PQ minister accused of theft in the one major store that had been an emblem of Anglo arrogance in the nationalist folklore (remember the saleslady yelling "Speak white" to Québécois customers), and many were to float the idea that Eaton's was acting out of vengeance for the humiliation of having to abide by Bill 101. It was even suggested that Charron had been framed. Only this time, the culprit-as-victim charade did not fly. A tearful Charron had to go. Here was a man who had a very promising future, squandering it away by committing a theft worthy of a teenager, saying that he could no longer take the pressure and wanted to be a normal human being again. A man longing for non-responsibility, behaving like an adolescent. Like his role model and father figure, René Lévesque himself.

CHAPTER TWENTY-FIVE

More Trouble

Imagine that you are a provincial government in Canada whose raison d'être is to secede from the federation, and that you have failed to achieve this. In times gone by, when pleading with a citizenry in a foul mood for some reason or other, you could always resort to the argument that if things were not going so well now, everything would be so much better after the province had become a separate country. That avenue is now closed, at least for the moment.

All you are left with is the task of governing like any other provincial government. Pretty boring stuff if you were dreaming of having diplomats at your beck and call who would negotiate international conventions on your behalf, as well as a small but respectable army that could take part in peacemaking operations, in Haiti, for example, or in some other country you could afford to send troops to. That dream is over. You will not be getting calls from the White House. No big speech at the United Nations Assembly for you either. Your own citizenry has said no to all of that, and what you will do from now on is, among other things, establish the fees for fishing licences, as well as manage schools, hospitals, roads, bridges, and so on and so forth. Depressing? Yes.

Now imagine you are the head of that government and that not only has your goal eluded you, but your arch enemy has managed to succeed where you failed. Indeed, Pierre Trudeau's Canada had come into its own with the patriation of the Constitution and the addition of the Charter of Rights and Freedoms. Both Lévesque and Trudeau had dreamed of emancipating their country once and for all; in striving to attain his goal, Lévesque had only given Trudeau an opportunity to try harder and make a go of it. Lévesque must have been the most miserable man in Quebec.

Now, the PQ had promised good government, something that can be gratifying if the economy co-operates. It did not. Canada was in the throes of a terrible recession. Unemployment was up, and so was the number of welfare recipients; provincial revenues were down, so there was little money to launch exciting new programs. The PQ thought the situation could not get any worse. It did.

The provincial deficit was then $3 billion yearly. Quebec's credit rating was in serious jeopardy. In order to put the province back on its fiscal feet, the government had no choice but to cut expenses. That meant reducing salaries in the public sector, an item that accounted for 52 percent of the overall budget. Risky as it would be politically, the Lévesque government felt that they had to try, and they paid dearly for it.

The Quiet Revolution had marked the ascent of a new socio-economic class, public servants—there were now almost three hundred thousand of them—whose median income was almost one-third higher than similar workers in the private sector. They had done even better under a PQ bent on reinforcing the state on all fronts. True, their union leadership was ideologically close to the PQ, but union leaders are politicians. They have to get elected too. Co-operating with the government in reducing salaries in order to bring down the deficit would have been tantamount to political suicide for any of them. So when the government launched a new round of negotiations with public sector unions with the avowed aim of reducing salaries for the sake of fiscal responsibility and social solidarity, all labour leaders screamed bloody murder, of course. The government's chief negotiator was a young, ambitious lawyer from the Saguenay by the name of Lucien Bouchard. He got nowhere.

On December 11, 1982, government legislated cutbacks that amounted to 20 percent of the public payroll. And as if that were not enough, that same day members of the

National Assembly voted themselves a 6 percent salary hike. Adroit timing, indeed. All hell broke loose. There were strikes and demonstrations galore. No pay? Okay, no work. Firefighters would play cards instead of responding to emergencies; the sick were left without care in hospitals; school kids were treated to numerous holidays. It was pure chaos. Strikers were emboldened enough to molest PQ ministers en route to the weekly Cabinet meeting. Even René Lévesque was roundly booed everywhere he went.

The atmosphere went from bad to worse. On January 28, 1983, thirty-three thousand public servants took to the streets in Quebec City. Some protesters brandished signs calling Lévesque "The Butcher of New Carlisle," a ridiculous reference to Nazi tormentor Klaus Barbie, who was then being tried in France for torturing and murdering Jean Moulin, the head of the French Resistance, in 1943. It was curious that this should happen to the man who had made a career of importing foreign political references to Quebec, although not all of them very apt. It was like being bitten by the dog you have sicced on someone else. According to witnesses close to Lévesque, that one hurt.

In short, 1982 and 1983 were years of bitter discontent. There was talk of little else in Quebec, and whatever measures the government introduced to mitigate the bad economic situation, it was never enough for it to regain any semblance of popularity. In fairness to the PQ government, it must be said that they were trying hard to improve things. For instance, they launched a program to encourage home ownership, Corvée-Habitation, which was successful. Thousands of Québécois families thus were able to own their own home for the first time, a feat that had eluded their parents.

As well, in one now well-known case, Lévesque personally overturned a decision made by his cultural affairs minister, Clément Richard, who had nixed a subsidy of $300,000 to a group of young street performers adept at walking on stilts and breathing fire. Thanks to Lévesque's grant, they eventually formed a little company. Today, Cirque du Soleil is a mega entertainment business worth billions of dollars, with thousands of employees and a very enviable worldwide reputation. Lévesque's initiative went almost unnoticed at the time, but one can safely say that his stroke of luck in the case of the Cirque summed up his whole economic credo: that the state should use its financial clout, although modestly so, to unleash Quebec's creativity and allow it to flourish internationally. The Cirque's venture was a very wise use of taxpayer money, but then, how often will the state be that lucky? Unfortunately for Lévesque, he did not live long enough to witness the Cirque's astounding success.

What to do then in those times of economic hardship? Travel? He tried that, but it only seemed to worsen things. He tried again to charm American audiences in Chicago and San Francisco, to no avail. He went to France, but he still did not like France, and all he seemed to do was to enrage French protocol officials. He tried Italy, a safe target. Rome, the pope ... He bombed there, too. First, after having had a warm chat with the president of Italy, Sandro Pertini, he had the gall to reveal to the press what the president had confided in him, namely that Pertini was not too impressed with the current leadership in Ottawa, that is, Pierre Trudeau. Pertini was so furious that he publicly rebuked Lévesque and turned down an official invitation to Quebec. Then the premier went to the Vatican, and René Lévesque being René Lévesque, he did not even refrain from smoking in the presence of His Holiness. That is when the French-language press really got on his back—and stayed there.

He was no better with foreign visitors. When Robert Mugabe came calling, Lévesque compared the departure of Anglo Quebecers to the exodus of whites in Zimbabwe. A most unfortunate comparison, you would have to say. And then, in a later trip to Japan, he compared the Quebec people to the Palestinians. The poor man couldn't seem to help himself. Having rejected Canada in his heart long ago, then having failed to convince his fellow citizens to form a country of their own, he was left frantically borrowing fragments of identity from other nationalities totally foreign to Quebec.

The PQ government really entered hard-luck territory on May 8, 1984, when a corporal in the Canadian Forces by the name of Denis Lortie forced his way into the National Assembly, shooting with a semi-automatic pistol and killing three people. His aim, he confessed later, was to "destroy the Lévesque government." Insanity had reached new heights. Lévesque was crushed. Anyone would have been.

The surest sign that a government is on its last legs is when its members say they want to leave public office in order to "spend more time with their family." Lévesque lost two important ministers, Pierre Marois and Jacques-Yvan Morin, who just could not take it anymore. His inner circle of advisers started thinning, too, and they were replaced by able but less experienced people. Things had gotten so bad that even Trudeau's departure from public life in 1984 did not bring a smile to Lévesque's face.

The return to power of the federal Progressive Conservatives under the leadership of Brian Mulroney, who had managed to snag fifty-two ridings in Quebec, seemed to hold some promise for the future. Lévesque thought that

Mulroney's installation at 24 Sussex, which was due to the support of so many soft nationalist voters, would enhance co-operation between Quebec and Ottawa. That new spirit of understanding, he hoped, would put him in better stead with voters.

Lévesque was wrong. Again.

CHAPTER TWENTY-SIX

The Debacle

With the ideal of secession put on the back burner for a long, long time, the PQ's erstwhile dominant stream of idealists had been slowly but surely overtaken by another current, this one made up of pragmatic politicians in Lévesque's mould whose sole aim was to retain power. They were good at interpreting polls and reading the general public, as real politicians do. And what they saw was not good. The appetite for independence had almost disappeared from the political map; the desire for a milder version of it, in the form of sovereignty, was barely visible. What Quebecers wanted, above all, was peace with Ottawa, more concord, no more fighting. And any party bent on more bickering with the federal government—now headed by the amiable Brian Mulroney, a native son of Quebec who spoke French like a Québécois—was doomed at the ballot box.

The PQ then did what any party would do to get re-elected: they compromised, even on their raison d'être. In September 1984, a few weeks after Mulroney's election, Lévesque gave the first signs of a rapprochement when he came out of a Cabinet retreat at Fort-Prével with a casual remark, again based on a foreign reference, that had a distinct whiff of the peace pipe about it: "Canada is not the gulag." Cabinet had just resolved that there would be a moratorium on the pursuit of sovereignty. It was game over for the idealists in the PQ.

The movement gained some more momentum in October when Intergovernmental Affairs Minister Pierre Marc Johnson, widely seen as Lévesque's successor, gave a lengthy interview to *Le Devoir* in which he claimed that the objective of sovereignty should give way to a new concept, "national affirmation." Lévesque said nothing. Many took this to mean that the new orientation had the tacit approval of the premier. The general public seemed indifferent to the news, but the hardliners in the PQ realized quickly that the dream of their youth was dead.

The final blow came in November, when Lévesque explained his new position to the PQ leadership. We must give the federal government its "proverbial last chance," he wrote, adding that "sovereignty was no longer the supreme insurance policy" it used to be. "Now what form will take this Nation-State, that we thought was so near, I have no idea." "That's it," lamented the remaining radicals, "now we know Lévesque is no longer with us, he has lost faith in our Sacred Cause." Predictably, things began to unravel.

THE FIRST TO GO were several backbenchers identified with the hardliners. They were followed by very important ministers, notably Camille Laurin and Jacques Parizeau. The shock wave was felt all over Quebec, and PQ militants were leaving the party in droves. It was a sort of replay of the "Night of the Long Knives" in that the pragmatist faction of the party had triumphed over the idealist faction—only it took the form of a slow-motion hara-kiri. At its January 1985 policy convention, the PQ discarded article 1 of its platform, the one calling for the sovereignty of Quebec, the very purpose of the party. The PQ was no longer the PQ.

In the meantime, everybody in Quebec witnessed the devastating effects all this was having on René Lévesque's personal life. He was drinking too much, skirt-chasing like a young stud fresh out of the seminary, and more disdainful of protocol than ever. His genius for words had begun to desert him. He would give long, rambling interviews that led nowhere; he sounded confused in his spontaneous speeches and in his answers in the National Assembly. Even within the PQ, respect for the old man was at its lowest ebb; backbenchers and ministers alike were not so discreetly whispering that the premier had lost it, that he would do the party a favour if he resigned. Lévesque responded by growing only more suspicious of his most trusted allies.

Even more ominous was a January 1985 holiday in the Caribbean that Lévesque cut short after a very bitter dispute with Corinne. Upon returning to Quebec, he resumed the hard drinking, and his behaviour took such a bizarre turn that his entourage forcibly took him to a hospital in Quebec City. People around him were sick with worry. Was he gravely ill? Was he going through a depression? After a short stay at the hospital, where he was able to rest a little and was submitted to a battery of tests, Lévesque came out with a clean bill of health but a wounded soul. René Lévesque was no longer René Lévesque.

On the night of June 20, 1985, when members of the National Assembly were celebrating the end of the session, they were stunned to hear that Lévesque had resigned. He had not even bothered to advise his caucus, and no one knew where he was. That was how disgusted the man was.

CHAPTER TWENTY-SEVEN

An Abundance of Ironies

Lévesque's departure was greeted with more than the usual concert of kudos reserved for retiring politicians. People everywhere knew there was something historical about his departure; rarely had the passing of an era been so palpable. The only comparable event was, well, the resignation of Pierre Trudeau. In Quebec feelings oscillated between mourning and relief. In English Canada, the announcement elicited statement after statement of respect and affection, a homage as strange as the land itself, given the man's secessionist ambitions. But both linguistic communities agreed on his worthiest contribution to public life: the sense of self-confidence emanating from French-speaking Quebec thanks to the resolute actions of a short man who sometimes had doubt etched all over his face.

Instilling self-confidence in Quebecers had indeed been the first objective of Lévesque's political crusade. In 1985 he was leaving behind a French Quebec where the majority no longer felt intimidated by the English-speaking minority, thanks in part to Bill 101. French-speaking Quebecers were buying their own homes in record numbers; young Québécois were now flooding business and engineering schools; in every domain of activity, there was a sense of purpose, a desire to achieve, that previous generations had never dreamed of. Life had changed in the province, for the better. Pierre Trudeau had proved to Quebecers that they could succeed in Canada; Lévesque had proved to them that they could succeed in Quebec. Irony of ironies, it was precisely because his fellow citizens felt better about themselves that they could do without Lévesque's other great political objective: independence. The man had failed here because he had succeeded there.

In fact, the only ones who were happy to see Lévesque go were the radicals à la Pierre Bourgault. They accused the outgoing premier of having killed the idea of Quebec's independence with his sovereignist alternative. A charge most unfair, since any Québécois could still dream of an independent state, but, as Lévesque knew instinctively right from the start, those committed to that ideal never amounted to more than 15 percent of the French-speaking population (an estimate that was, and still is, very generous). With his sovereignty-association project, Lévesque had rescued the idea of independence from the political wilderness to which it seemed condemned forever and thus found the needed impetus to reach power. And once in office, the Parti Québécois had been at least able to implement many of its social democrat objectives, a feat impossible to achieve without the exercise of power.

The malcontents should rather have bemoaned the fact that Lévesque had unwittingly strengthened Trudeau's hand in imposing Canada's new constitutional order. Pierre Trudeau had brilliantly used Lévesque's sovereignty threat to fulfill his own dream of a Canada where the rights of the individual would coexist peacefully with the responsibilities of the state. Lévesque had said many times that he did not want to destroy Canada but to change it, and if his sovereignty plan had come to pass, indeed, Canada would have been changed. But then the transformation of Canada was a secondary aim for him; it was something that would occur almost as an afterthought.

If René Lévesque had been less Quebec-obsessed and had really wanted to change Canada, he would easily have found allies in other provinces, at least among the many politicians who shared his social democrat ideas. A good case in point was B.C.'s NDP premier Dave Barrett, who visited Lévesque in Montreal soon after he was elected in 1972. Barrett was sure to find a soulmate in Lévesque, and indeed, the two got on famously, having similar ideas in economic and social matters. But Lévesque never pursued the dialogue with Barrett. His thoughts and actions were too Quebec-centred to allow it, and he must have sensed that the rank-and-file members of the PQ no doubt would have balked. If Lévesque had made some allies among the other socially progressive politicians after the 1980 referendum debacle, he could have stopped Trudeau's constitutional juggernaut in 1981 or at least got some deal to his advantage. But his interest in Canada was so weak that he did not even try to find allies, whereas Trudeau had reached out and found support outside of Ottawa. Alone and left to his own devices, Lévesque was sure to fail and had failed.

There was another almost insurmountable force that Lévesque had never reckoned with: history. Time and time again, he had deplored the fact that Canada had become a federation instead of remaining a true confederation. But no one could set the clock back to 1867, and as one shrewd observer of Canadian affairs, General de Gaulle no less, had once observed, "Every confederation tends to become a federation: to wit, the United States and Canada." In the end, the Québécois did not believe in independence, and still do not, and René Lévesque never found in him the strength to believe in a renewed Canada, whereas Trudeau did. Which explains why Lévesque's failure became Trudeau's success.

OF ALL THE IMAGES of Lévesque departing, one stands out, again thanks to the very observant Don Macpherson of *The Gazette,* an image that the French-language press completely missed.

A "roast" had been organized in Montreal, on October 4, 1985, to pay tribute to René Lévesque. In keeping with the best traditions of this saturnal rite North American politicians are so fond of, fine food was abundant, liquor flowed, and so did lengthy, not always moving testimonies and tasteless jokes.

There was one man in the room who did not understand a single word, since it was a French-only evening, but endured it all very patiently. He was Joseph Keleutak, the president of the Regional Administration Kativik, who had travelled fourteen hundred kilometres from Kuujjuaq to attend the event and bring a gift from the Inuit to Lévesque, a soapstone sculpture showing a woman making braids out of a sealskin. Keleutak's presence was quite fitting, since René Lévesque, as minister of natural resources, had been instrumental in opening schools in the North where instruction would be given in Native languages. As premier, determined to give the Aboriginal minorities exactly the same tools he wanted for the French majority of Quebec, he had done much to provide First Nations with their institutions of governance—school boards, regional health authorities, economic development mechanisms—and this at a time when Aboriginal self-government was still only a concept just about everywhere else in Canada.

All of a sudden, something unplanned happened. The end of the evening was near, Lévesque had just been madly applauded on stage, and he was returning to his seat. Then he turned around suddenly, went back to the stage, took the microphone, and asked the Inuit official to join him. With Keleutak standing beside him, Lévesque, using English because it was the only language he shared with the man, invited him to say a few words in Inuktitut. Keleutak obliged and made a short speech that, this time, he alone could understand. The crowd gave him and Lévesque a standing ovation.

Let us savour the moment. Two men applauded on stage, both flesh, blood, and soul, like all of us. One who represents the First Peoples of the Earth, whose arts, sciences, and beliefs quietly permeate our everyday life. An Inuit, a member of that most ingenious nation that has triumphed over cold, hunger, and darkness and has enriched all known languages of the planet with a word that needs no translation: *kayak,* a word that conjures up both nautical locomotion and Olympic sportsmanship. A people with a memory and a language of their own, who never needed a state to assert their distinctiveness. Beside him, a man who embodies a historical anomaly of the highest order: the novel-like story of the French-speakers of America, with their voice still audible after three centuries of existence, with their own memory and language. A people with a state of their own, Quebec, and a country they share with the First Nations and so many other cultures. Canada, more a continent than a country. Two men like the rest of us, each a testimony to cultural resilience, both of them the living promise of a future as rich and as diverse as the rest of the country.

It was one of those rare moments where History morphs into Poetry.

CHAPTER TWENTY-EIGHT

Two Statues

René Lévesque was felled by a heart attack a little more than two years later, on November 1, 1987. On the next day, Prime Minister Brian Mulroney had the Canadian flag flown at half-mast.

Not much had happened in between. Lévesque had travelled around the world and finally visited some of the countries he had wanted Quebec to emulate, Denmark and Sweden, for instance. He had written his memoirs, which had brought him a measure of wealth. He was active again as a journalist and political commentator. He had bought a condominium on Montreal's Nuns' Island and was finally enjoying life with Corinne, away from the rough and tough world of politics. Of course, he remained as unfaithful as ever, but she no longer paid attention.

Two months after Lévesque's departure, the PQ, now led by Pierre Marc Johnson, was defeated by Quebec's comeback kid, Robert Bourassa, and his Liberals. But Lévesque did not care anymore. He had a life now.

I saw him at a book launch at our publisher's, Québec/Amérique, in Montreal, a few weeks before his death. He was well dressed, looking healthy and rested, but I could never get near him. He was besieged by admirers as usual, beloved right till the end.

Thousands paid him homage at Montreal's Notre Dame basilica. Pierre Trudeau was there. Even Pierre Bourgault was sad to see him go. After the hearse left the church for Quebec City, where the state funeral and the burial were to take place, the crowd spontaneously broke into Lévesque's favourite song, "Gens du pays." A funeral, and they were singing … Where else but in Quebec?

RENÉ LÉVESQUE'S MEMORY is still very much alive. Every time politicians pass laws attempting to free the political process from occult money, they quote Lévesque's example. The man wanted to be remembered first and foremost as a democrat, and in that regard, he achieved his dream. As for Quebec sovereignty, well …

He is far from gone in that regard, too. Much to the chagrin of the remaining and aging diehard separatists, Lévesque is still in charge of the PQ. To wit, every time a PQ leadership contender pushes for independence pure and simple, that person is either not elected or, if elected, has to backtrack at lightning speed when polls show that he or she is heading for political oblivion. And every PQ leader has to sing the praises of the founding father to acquire any semblance of legitimacy. "Monsieur Lévesque" still is the boss, still the man, "oui, monsieur." Independence is not on the horizon; sovereignty may be, although again, with a strong dose of Canada. In other words, Lévesque's adolescent pipe dream lives on while the rest of Quebec ages and matures.

But that's all right. Politicians still get elected under the PQ banner all the same. They get elected democratically, and nothing else counts. That's what Lévesque taught them all. The rest is history, or literature, take your pick.

TWO STATUES commemorate his passage among us. One is in Quebec City, near the National Assembly, taller than the man himself, very official and proper in its design, resembling more a distant cousin who did well in life.

I prefer the one that was erected in his native New Carlisle. It shows the real René Lévesque, the one everybody loved and respected, with his mischievous smile and his smokeless cigarette. There is just one problem: the statue has its back to the ever-beautiful Gaspesian sea of his childhood.

René Lévesque deserved better.

René Lévesque is in a class of his own when it comes to sources. No other provincial premier in Canadian history has elicited as many full-length books, feature articles, and essays. No other premier has been as much talked about either, with the possible exception of Newfoundland and Labrador's Joey Smallwood. And as for television series about his life and times, though none of them are very good in my opinion, René Lévesque again knows no equal; the numerous radio and TV documentaries on him are of much better quality.

The bulk of my sources were in French, as one would expect, and to those who are conversant in that language, I must recommend Pierre Godin's masterful four-tome biography: I. *L'enfant du siècle,* II. *Héros malgré lui,* III. *L'espoir et le chagrin,* and IV. *L'homme brisé.* To him I owe all the percentages and figures quoted in my book. Also of note here is Radio-Canada's stellar radio series *Point de mire sur René Lévesque,* a riveting audio document that, I hope, will be emulated for other great political figures. And if you want to know more about Quebec's recent history, you will benefit from Pierre Duchesne's biography of Jacques Parizeau; Martine Tremblay's memoirs; Jean-François

Nadeau's *Bourgault;* and just about every book written by Lévesque's premier strategist, Claude Morin.

As for books either written in or translated into English, Peter Desbarats's *René: A Canadian in Search of a Country,* published in 1977, and Graham Fraser's *PQ: René Lévesque and the Parti Québécois in Power,* published in 1984, remain surprisingly relevant and insightful, a testament to the immense talent of these two journalists. I must especially thank Graham Fraser for his account of Lesage's coming to power and of the 1981 constitutional negotiations. For Quebec's twentieth-century history, the best read in translation remains Marcel Trudel's *Memoirs of a Less Travelled Road.* Unfortunately, Trudel's *Mythes et réalités dans l'histoire du Québec* is available in French only, as are Georges-Émile Lapalme's and Gérard Filion's memoirs.

Thanks to the very helpful staff at the Library of Parliament in Ottawa, chief among them Louis Branchaud, I was able to read every newspaper and magazine article ever written about Lévesque. The one source that stands out here for me is *The Gazette*'s Don Macpherson: always deep, witty, and a joy to read. I figure Don now owes us a book on the exhilarating years he reported on.

ACKNOWLEDGMENTS

Every time he had just published a book, my good friend
Matt Cohen (now deceased) used to say that he felt
unemployed. That was precisely how I was feeling when
John Ralston Saul, the initiator of this Extraordinary
Canadians series, approached me to write about René
Lévesque. The next day, I was busy researching my subject
and making notes, having forgotten all about my latest novel
and my fleeting glory as a Giller Prize nominee. So I want to
say, Thank you, John. Your trust in me nourished my confidence during the year it took me to write this book. Now I
feel unemployed again, but this time, I don't mind as much.

Although the first draft of this biographical essay was
written in French, I must underline the fact that the English
version is in no way a translation. As soon as I was done with
the French text, I set about writing it anew in English. Those
who are able to compare them will see how different the two
books are, even though they deal with the same subject and
the same facts. It was quite an exhilarating literary experience. Now, because English is my second *langue officielle,* I
had to recruit some outside help, especially when it came to
mastering the use of English prepositions. My two dear and
long-time friends Cindy Runzer and Linda Wiens, both, like

myself, parliamentary interpreters, came to my rescue here, as did my editor at Penguin, Diane Turbide. John Ralston Saul's comments on the first draft were also very helpful. To the four of them, my heartfelt thanks.

For the French version, my editor at Boréal, Jean Bernier, as usual, played the role of the devil's advocate and provided me with his customary sound guidance. My son Gabriel and my friend Monique Perrin d'Arloz were also very helpful with their remarks.

For both versions of the book, I benefited immensely from the encouragement of the woman I love, Monique Léger. All the while supervising the renovations at our new home in Parrsboro, Nova Scotia, she took the time to read the work in progress and comment on it. I guess that's what you call multi-tasking. Me, I only write.

It should be no wonder that I, the novelist, should write about politics too. After all, I am the son of a political journalist who was also a man of letters in his own right, the late Jean-Marc Poliquin. He was Radio-Canada's bureau chief in Ottawa for many years. Growing up with a father who was a professional commentator on politics as well as a Flaubert aficionado was my writing school, and it only stands to reason that my *Lévesque* be dedicated to him.

1922   René Lévesque is born August 24 in Campbellton,
        New Brunswick. He spends his early years in New
        Carlisle, in the Gaspé Peninsula.

1937   His father, Dominique, dies on the operating
        table. His mother remarries four months later and
        moves her family to Quebec City.

1941   Lévesque graduates with a B.A. and enters the law
        school at Université Laval.

1944   After being expelled from law school, he joins the
        U.S. Office of War Information as a broadcaster.
        In July, he lands in Normandy and later hooks up
        with General Patton's Third United States Army.
        He is then seconded to General Patch's Seventh
        United States Army for the Alsace campaign.

1945   In March 1945, he is in Germany and witnesses
        the liberation of the Dachau concentration camp.
        The war ends May 8, and Lévesque is back in
        Montreal in October. In November, he is hired as
        an announcer at La Voix du Canada, Radio-
        Canada's international service.

1947   He marries Louise L'Heureux. They will have
        three children: Pierre, 1948; Claude, 1950; and
        Suzanne, 1956.

1951   He spends three months in Korea as a war corre-
        spondent and establishes his credentials as a
        serious journalist.

1957   René Lévesque leaves radio for television, where
        he is given his own current affairs program, *Point
        de mire* (Focal Point), which propels him to
        stardom in Quebec.

1958   On December 29, Radio-Canada's producers go
        on strike. Lévesque joins the ensuing protest
        movement. This event marks the birth of his
        political persona.

1959   The strike ends in March. His contract at *Point de
        mire* is not renewed. He moves to private radio.
        On September 7, Maurice Duplessis, leader of the
        Union Nationale and Quebec's premier-for-life,
        dies. He had been in power for fifteen years.

1960   Lévesque joins the Quebec Liberal Party and agrees
        to run in the June 22 election. He is elected in the
        riding of Laurier. The Liberals win the election.
        Jean Lesage becomes premier. Lévesque is soon

thereafter appointed minister for hydroelectric resources and public works, where he institutes the practice of calling for tenders for any government contract over $25,000, a first in Quebec.

1961   He takes over the new Ministry of Natural Resources, which combines two portfolios, Mines and Hydroelectric Resources. He right away begins planning the nationalization of Quebec's electricity under the umbrella of Hydro-Québec.

1962   Lesage and his Cabinet give Lévesque the go-ahead for the nationalization of electricity. The Liberal Party is re-elected with a stronger majority.

1963   The Front de libération du Québec (FLQ), a terrorist organization whose aim was to liberate Quebec by violent means, is created. They undertake bombings and "financing" hold-ups.

1965   Following a Cabinet shuffle, Lévesque loses his Natural Resources portfolio and is appointed minister for family and welfare.

1966   On June 5, Lesage's Liberal government is defeated by Daniel Johnson's Union Nationale. Lévesque retains his seat in the Legislative Assembly.

1967   On July 24, at Expo 67, General de Gaulle shouts
        "Vive le Québec libre" from the balcony of
        Montreal's City Hall. On October 13, Lévesque,
        now a proponent of sovereignty-association for
        Quebec, leaves the Quebec Liberal Party.

1968   On April 19, Lévesque launches a new party
        devoted to his ideal, the Mouvement Souveraineté-
        Association (MSA). In that same month, Pierre
        Elliott Trudeau is elected leader of the Liberal Party
        of Canada, effectively succeeding Lester B. Pearson
        as prime minister. On June 25, Prime Minister
        Trudeau wins his first general election. On
        October 11, the MSA merges with another
        separatist party, the Ralliement national, to form
        the Parti Québécois (PQ). Days before, the other
        major separatist party, the Rassemblement pour
        l'indépendance nationale (RIN), headed by Pierre
        Bourgault, disbands at the leadership's behest.
        Bourgault joins the PQ and urges his comrades to
        do the same. The separatist forces are now united
        under Lévesque's leadership.

1970   On April 29, in its first electoral contest, the PQ
        totals 23 percent of the popular vote and wins
        seven seats in the National Assembly. Robert

Bourassa's Liberal Party is now in power. Lévesque himself is defeated. He returns to journalism as a columnist for the *Journal de Montréal*. He has left his family and now lives with Corinne Côté, whom he will marry in 1978. On October 5, James Richard Cross, Great Britain's trade commissioner in Montreal, is abducted by an FLQ cell. This marks the beginning of the October Crisis. Soon thereafter, Quebec's labour minister, Pierre Laporte, is kidnapped by another FLQ cell. On October 16, at the request of the Quebec National Assembly and of the authorities of the City of Montreal, the federal government enacts the War Measures Act. On the next day, October 17, Laporte's body is found in the trunk of a car in Saint-Hubert, south of Montreal.

1973   The PQ is defeated once more in the October 29 general election by Bourassa's Liberals. So is Lévesque. The PQ garners 35 percent of the vote but elects only six MNAs. After the debacle, the PQ engages in years of soul-searching, with the result that they resolve to first get elected on a good-government platform and to then have a referendum on Quebec's sovereignty.

1976   On November 15, the PQ defeats the Liberal
Party and forms the government. Also elected is
René Lévesque, the new premier of Quebec.

1977   On August 26, the National Assembly passes
Bill 101 to ensure the predominance of the French
language in Quebec.

1980   The referendum on Quebec's sovereignty takes
place on May 20. The No side wins with
59.56 percent of the vote; the Yes side garners
40.44 percent.

1981   In early November, Trudeau manages to convince
the first ministers to patriate the Canadian
Constitution from London and to add to it a
Charter of Rights and Freedoms. Lévesque is left
out of the deal, to which he could not have acqui-
esced in the first place. He and his cohort will
christen that episode the "Night of the Long
Knives." In December, a radicalized and angry PQ
puts forward a resolution to reject the idea of
association with Canada, and Lévesque immediately threatens to quit politics if the resolution is
not reversed. An internal referendum is soon
organized, and Lévesque wins with 95 percent of

the vote. But the consultation is dubbed the "renérendum."

1984   Trudeau leaves politics in June. Brian Mulroney's Progressive Conservatives come to power in Ottawa in September. Lévesque now thinks of effecting a rapprochement with the federal government, much to the consternation of many of his comrades-in-arms. The PQ begins to unravel.

1985   Lévesque quits politics on June 20.

1987   On November 1, René Lévesque dies in Montreal of a heart attack. He is buried in Quebec City.